ANIMALS

— AS —

TEACHERS

— & —

HEALERS

▲

true stories & reflections

▼

SUSAN CHERNAK McELROY

FOREWORD BY MICHAEL W. FOX

BALLANTINE BOOKS
New York

A Ballantine Book
Published by The Random House Publishing Group

Copyright © 1996, 1997 by Susan Chernak McElroy
Foreword copyright © 1997 by Michael W. Fox

Published in the United States by Ballantine Books, an imprint of The Random House Publishing Group, a division of Random House, Inc., New York, and simultaneously in Canada by Random House of Canada Limited, Toronto. Originally published in slightly different form by NewSage Press in 1996.

Ballantine and colophon are registered trademarks of Random House, Inc.

www.ballantinebooks.com

Library of Congress Catalog Card Number: 97-97061

ISBN: 0-345-42117-5

Cover photo © Daniel J. Cox/Tony Stone Images, NY

Manufactured in the United States of America

First Ballantine Books Trade Edition: March 1998

6 8 10 9 7

For the two men in my life who have loved me
without condition or limit:
my father, the late Julius Chernak,
and my cherished husband and partner,
Leslie James McElroy

How are we to build a new humanity? Reverence for life.
Existence depends more on reverence for life than the law and
    the prophets.
Reverence for life comprises the whole ethic of love in its
    deepest and highest sense.
It is the source of constant renewal for the individual and for
    mankind.

—ALBERT SCHWEITZER
Reverence for Life

CONTENTS

Contents

ACKNOWLEDGMENTS

I have felt from the beginning that this was not my book, but rather, that it was given to me to do. The task was assigned by the universe, not because I am a gifted writer (I consider myself adequate at best) or because I love animals better than most (I carry my share of guilt over the animals in my care). My single most important contribution to the creation of this book is my determination that such a book needed to be in the world. As a result, dozens of "angels" heard me and were inspired by my enthusiasm. Friends and family cheered me on, people sent in beautiful stories—the jewels of the book—from all over the world. I am grateful to the editors, book designers, and photographers, who gave the book life, form, and style. In particular, photographers Jodi Frediani, Craig Solin, and Sumner W. Fowler offered endearing images of our animal friends.

Most of all, my editor and first publisher, Maureen R. Michelson—a woman of vision—nursed the text through grueling drafts, compelling me with her clarity and critical eye to look closely at what I was saying. Her yellow Post-its stuck like burrs to every page I wrote, challenging me. To Maureen, I owe this book. That it is here and solid and good is a tribute to her great patience and amazing artistry with words on paper. I would also like to acknowledge my copy editor, Tracy Smith, for her attention to detail and professionalism.

My mother, Hermine Chernak, read pieces of the first draft and did what every daughter prays for in such a moment: she cried, tears streaming down her cheeks. Then she looked up at me with an expression of absolute awe. That is the gift my mother gave me—a gift that sustained me through rewrite after rewrite: The deep sweetness of a mother's adoration that, when remembered, fills up the soul when it runs temporarily dry.

Many magazines and organizations took up my original call for stories and spread the word: *Dog Fancy*, *Cat Fancy*, *Horse Illustrated*, The Delta Society, Green Chimneys, The Humane Society of the United States, and *Reflections Magazine*. In reading the nationally published requests, countless local humane and animal rescue/rehabilitation organizations also spread the word to their local members. The groundswell of support has been overwhelming and I am deeply indebted to all the organizations and magazines that made space for my plea for stories.

From those resources, many of which I am unaware, the stories came. The hundreds who sent their stories to me transformed my life and my thoughts over the past two years. Each story offered me a fresh way of seeing, a new idea, a flush of energy when I needed it most, a deep moment of reflection, of recognition. Their words carried me from what I had thought about animals in my life to what I knew about animals as teachers and healers. Without these people, without their willingness to share feelings and moments that were so personal, there would be no book. I am indebted to each and every one. That I could not include all of the stories is in no way a reflection of their worth, but of the frustrating confines of space and time.

I am deeply grateful to Michael W. Fox and Michael Tobias, whose words and writings continue to inspire and encourage me, ever challenging me to broaden my thinking and expand my heart. These generous men have taken my book by the hand and helped it find its way into the world. Both are eloquent and passionate spokesmen for what I pray will be a new and coming consciousness of "whole-i-ness" and loving communion among the living beings of the earth.

I also want to acknowledge my family and friends for sharing and laughing with me. The older I get, the more I understand that the life force that sustains us all grows and blossoms most powerfully in relationships: Julius and Nancy Chernak, Leslie Chernak ("Cuz"), Keith Smith, Joe Kogel, C.J. Mitchell, Mom and Kim McElroy, Claire Melde, Maureen Keenan-Mason, Kyle Brown, and Mike Ruggieri.

And lastly, a soul-felt thanks to my steadfast and loving partner, my familiar—my beloved Arrow.

I am very grateful for this book and for the opportunity to write something about it. Susan McElroy has compiled a unique and moving testimony of the gifts that animals have bestowed on their human companions, some life-saving, others life-sustaining and truly miraculous. The ultimate goal of this book is to elevate the status and significance of animals in society, which is long overdue for the good of the animals and, as this book so ably demonstrates, for the good of humanity.

I have been a veterinarian since 1962 and I have been with the Humane Society of the United States for almost twenty years. Every day I see in one form or another animal abuse. Because we have become so emotionally disconnected from animals, we treat them as though they are unfeeling machines and disposable commodities. This reality reflects what seems to be a serious and growing human malady. Our lack of respect for animals and nature reflects a deep spiritual disorder in our species. I believe this is the primary cause of many physical and psychological diseases that afflict us today, and which no amount of animal experimentation or wonder drugs will prevent.

As a veterinarian, I am concerned about the health and

well-being of all creatures. For me the best medicine is the prevention of animal stress and suffering. The best way to accomplish this is to help reconnect people emotionally and spiritually with animals. The human/animal bond needs to be healed for the benefit of the animals and for our own good, as well. It is a rare book like *Animals as Teachers & Healers* that gives me some hope that this reconnection is being more widely recognized—and it is quickening.

I do have a strong sense of urgency, not because "time is running out," but because history repeats itself and suffering intensifies so long as our spiritual disconnectedness from the rest of Creation worsens. As Albert Schweitzer advised, "Until he extends his circle of compassion to include all living things, man himself will not find peace."

In earlier times, people recognized and respected animals as kin, as living relations of the same Creation sharing the same earth. Through such kinship, animals were our totems, familiars, and healers long before they were ever domesticated. I agree with the conclusion of some historians that the Biblical "fall" of humankind began with the domestication of animals and their domination, exploitation, and treatment as objects and mere commodities.

Yet the implicit instructions in the Book of Genesis are for people to "dress and to keep" all of God's Creation in reverential respect. The word "dominion" in Genesis is often interpreted as divine sanction for all forms of animal abuse. But the original meaning of the word "dominion" comes from the Hebrew verb *yorade*, which means to come down to; to have communion with and compassion for.

Native American elder David Monongye wrote a letter to the United Nations, urging the leaders of all nations to consider the wisdom of obedience to what Native Americans call our "original instructions." He advised, "The original instructions of the Creator are universal and valid for all time. The essence of these instructions is compassion for all life and love for all creation. We must realize that we do not live in a world of dead matter, but in a universe of living spirit. Let us open our eyes to the sacredness of Mother Earth, or our eyes will be opened for us."

Animals as Teachers & Healers opens our eyes to the immense powers and gifts that animals bestow upon us when we treat them according to our original instructions. Animals transform our everyday lives, taking us outside of ourselves and into the here and now of their own being. And through their presence, we come to feel the divine presence that dwells within all Creation. As Dostoyevsky wrote, "When you love every creature, you will understand the mystery of God in created things." As our eyes are opened, we sense something angelic in animals and in each other. Animals encourage us toward communion with the sacred dimension of reality that is as empowering and healing as it is inspiring and affirming.

The revelations of those who have healed and re-established the ancient bond with animals are well documented in this book. *Animals as Teachers & Healers* is an antidote for a spiritually hungry society that has yet to realize the wisdom of compassion, and the gifts and powers of animals. It is a book of affirmation for all lovers of creatures "great and small," for all those who have ever been branded as irrational, sentimental

"Bambi-loving tree huggers." I hope that this book reaches many skeptics and those alienated from creatures and Creation. This book can show them what they are missing in their lives that money and power cannot buy.

—DR. MICHAEL W. FOX
Vice President
The Humane Society of the United States

Animals as Teachers & Healers

Sitting at the Table of Life

> We need another and a wiser and perhaps a more mythical concept of animals. . . . We patronize them for their incompleteness, for their tragic fate of having taken form so far below ourselves. And therein we err, and greatly err. For the animal shall not be measured by man. In a world older and more complete than ours they moved finished and complete, gifted with extensions of the senses we have lost or never attained, living by voices we shall never hear. They are not brethren, they are not underlings; they are other nations, caught with ourselves in the net of life and time, fellow prisoners of the splendor and travail of the earth.
>
> —HENRY BESTON
> *The Outermost House*

Simply, and unequivocally, I am an animal lover. For as long as I can remember, animals have captivated me. My childhood memories are filled with animals: puppies, injured birds, alley cats, Easter chicks, the turtle my brother brought home from camp—the list is long. As a toddler living in a ninth-story, New York City apartment, I would even take the fish my dad caught for dinner, swaddle them in dish towels, and lug them around the house. I called them my babies and rocked and cradled the fish until the oil was hot and I was forced to abandon them to the frying pan.

My mom and dad treated all the creatures in our home with the same respect and concern that they extended to my brother and me. It was only natural that I would think of animals as my siblings, children, or friends. And it was only natural that I would talk to them and listen to what they had to say. Of all the gifts my parents have given me, their acceptance and encouragement of my special bond with animals is by far the greatest. It is the gift that would save my life, over and over again.

In my early adult years, my steadfast affinity for animals was actually more a source of embarrassment than anything else as I realized that many of the people I knew felt nothing remotely similar. To be perfectly honest, my special relationship with animals was one I was often quick to dismiss or even to deny in the company of what I call "non-animal people."

It was only during the course of writing this book and submerging myself in the abiding wisdom of its stories that I have shaken off, at last, the final traces of my hesitancy at being known as "an animal lover." I fully accept the magic bond that so many people share with animals. There was a time when I considered many of the profound moments I'd had with animals as frivolous. That began to change when I was suddenly faced with cancer and a grim prognosis for recovery. During my cancer journey, in my search for methods and memories of healing, I finally began to acknowledge the tremendous inspiration and healing presence offered to me by the animals in my life: past and present, real and imagined. The animals who have touched my life were my most powerful and enduring teachers and healers.

My dog Keesha served as a special guide throughout my healing process, even though she had died many years before I was diagnosed with cancer. Her memory became a crucial source of strength for me as I faced my two cancer surgeries and then endured weeks of radiation treatments. After successfully completing my cancer treatments, I decided to write a long-overdue tribute to Keesha and acknowledge all that she had brought to my life. It took me two years to finish my story about Keesha and another year-and-a-half to get it published. All the inspirational magazines turned it down because it wasn't about angels or miracles or even people. It was about a dog.

When my article was finally published in a pet magazine as "The Angel Who Fetched," the reader response overwhelmed me. Within days of its publication, letters started pouring in from all over the world about "other angels": the lives they had changed, the teachings they had offered, and the love and mercy they had shared. Their personal stories helped to validate and to confirm my own deep connection with Keesha and the many other animals in my life.

At the time "The Angel Who Fetched" was published, I was living on a beautiful island in the Pacific Northwest. I had married, acquired two apartment-dwelling cats, and was part of a small but vital women's group that met each week to talk about our lives and commit to making our dreams a reality.

We called ourselves The Faerrie Queenes and agreed over tea and banana bread—lots of banana bread—that we would each unearth our life purpose and pledge ourselves to a series of goals that would help us to achieve it, no matter what.

My life purpose revealed itself instantly. What I wrote that May night in 1992 and taped into my Faerrie Queene journal is as current in this moment as it was when I wrote it— perhaps even more so:

> I will acknowledge the profound and continual role of animals in my life as angels, teachers, and healers. I will repay this special gift by caring for, writing about, and speaking on behalf of animals throughout the course of my life. I will work to heal the relationship between people and animals by fostering an awareness of the sacredness, specialness, and spirituality that is a natural component of the animal kingdom.

From the moment that I wrote down my life purpose and presented it to my women's group, I had the eerie sensation that I didn't choose it, but that it had chosen me. A part of me also began to believe that I had been spared death so that I could have a chance to express my purpose in some meaningful way.

The idea for a book about animals as teachers and healers came to me soon after in a hazy daydream. It was one of those inspired ideas that feels instantly right. From that moment on, I never doubted that the book was to be the next step on my continuing healing journey. So convinced was I of the merit of my book idea that I decided to attend a writers' conference where I would have the opportunity to speak with two literary agents. Fifteen dollars bought ten minutes of their time and wisdom. With animated enthusiasm, I told them about my idea and why I thought it was so important to bring this long-overdue message of hope and healing to print. Both agents told me just as quickly that those kinds of books didn't sell. Then they proceeded to take up the rest of my precious ten minutes telling me their own animal stories. One was about a certain, much-beloved dog, and another was of a horse that had fulfilled a dream for a cherished daughter. In fact, they ran over their time limits to tell me these stories. This convinced me. I left absolutely certain that my book was, indeed, a superb idea.

And for months it remained just that—an idea. Then, one fortuitous night in late winter, a friend showed up at my forty-second birthday party with a neighbor whom I had never met. The neighbor is a book publisher. I told her my idea and later gave her some sample stories. In three days she called me and said, "Let's do it."

That quickly, my vision for a book began to jell. In addition to my own experiences, I knew I wanted to collect stories from other people who recognized animals as teachers and healers in their lives. I immediately put out a call for stories through animal publications and organizations nationally. I distributed flyers to bookstores, veterinary hospitals, and animal-oriented gift shops. The news spread and people called me with amazing tales of healing, insight, and joy. I interviewed people who work with and for animals, and I was interviewed by several local papers. Letters and stories flowed in by the hundreds. Most were about animals people had lived with and loved for a long time. Some recounted moments of glimpsing wildlife in forests or meadows and how that led to profound insight.

Numerous letters gave simple tribute to the life of a pet, or described a happy moment, a favorite dog's best trick, the joy of living with a special cat. When these humble stories began to arrive, I first believed that I had not made myself clear in my request for really special experiences, life-changing events. But after receiving hundreds of these letters detailing quite ordinary events, I learned to read the magic between the lines. These were deep and transformative happenings—the dog's trick performed back in 1925 for a woman who still lovingly recalls the memory, the cat who shared a man's pillow each night for two decades, the family goat who somehow managed to escape every pasture fence. These ordinary moments moved and shaped lives.

Throughout the book I weave my own narrative and observations of animals as teachers and healers with these stories from others who also share special relationships with animals. At the end of each chapter I have included stories that can stand alone. These stories do not require introduction or enhancement, but instead are complete unto themselves, offering an insight, a truth, or a legendary tale of mythological proportions.

It is my sincerest hope that this book will awaken readers to a different, richer way of seeing the world and its many nations, both human and animal. Perhaps the teachers you are seeking have found you already and are nestled at your hearth or in your barn. An Oregon man who sent me the story about a red fox observed: "Your idea for gathering modern animal stories is a brilliant one. Such lore has been part of human culture forever—until just recently, that is. It will be amazing to see what power these tales of relationships and encounters will have. It will be good for us."

Thomas Moore writes about the soul's deep longing for a heartfelt sense of home. "The end of our maltreatment of nature may come only when we have discovered that this earth in all its particular places and presences, offers the soul relief from its aching search for a home." Animals can offer us a way home. In their innocence and wisdom, in their connection to the earth and its most ancient rhythms, they show us a way back to a home they have never left.

At a symposium on nature and spirit, Protestant theologian Sally McFague presented a modern look at our ancient notion of "dominion" over the Garden of Eden. She proposed that the devastating social, spiritual, and ecological problems we face today hinge on our refusal to sit down and "take our place in the scheme of things." Our intended place is not that of overlord or master, but one of a respectful and loving partnership. As McFague spoke, I imagined a large, round table where all the earth's creatures sit side by side in natural communion. In this sacred circle, no one presides over another. The empty seat at this table is ours—the seat we will take when we understand that participation, not domination, is the true path to our soul's home.

Nearly ten years after my initial cancer diagnosis and treatment, I am healthy and well in body and spirit. Better, in truth, than before my healing journey began. I owe that wellness in great part to the large family of animals in my life, those

living and those long dead. And now, with the completion of
this book, I am blessed with an extended family of hundreds
of animals whose teachings and healings guide me, and remind
me of their lessons as I ask the questions and make the choices
that shape my life. Whether living or dead, these animals leave
a legacy of wisdom and love for the willing of heart. All of
them made a special place for me at their table, a place where I
was invited to sit for awhile, to hear their stories, and to learn.
As you read the following chapters, I ask that you listen closely
for the whisper of animal voices extending their gracious invi-
tation to you. *Please, come to the table.*

—SUSAN CHERNAK MCELROY
Bright Star Farm, Oregon
August 1996

PHOTO: SUMNER W. FOWLER

CHAPTER ONE

In Partnership:

OUR ANIMAL COMPANIONS AND WORKMATES

I think I could turn and live with the animals
   they are so placid and self-contain'd.
I stand and look at them long and long.

They do not sweat and whine about their condition,
They do not lie awake in the dark and weep for their sins,
They do not make me sick discussing their duty to God,
Not one is dissatisfied, not one is demented with the
   mania of owning things,
Not one kneels to another, nor to his kind that lived
   thousands of years ago,
Not one is respectable or unhappy over the whole earth.

              —WALT WHITMAN
              Song of Myself

The animals who know us most intimately are our companion animals. By right of domestication, our dogs, cats,
horses, and livestock animals have a deep and ancient bond
with us that has survived centuries of evolution and change.
Any animal can serve as a teacher; however, our companion

animals—the ones who share our daily lives—offer us an entire lifetime of learning experiences as we watch them grow, thrive, fail, and die.

These animals who share our homes and our work have an uncanny and unparalleled way of seeing through all our false layers, allowing our more genuine selves to emerge. When we are alone with our animal companions we don't bother with the masks and the performances, the armoring and the pretense, that we cultivate and display for our loved ones, friends, and enemies. Around our animals, we are our truest selves. When our guard is down, our defenses soften and we can gently open ourselves to receive love, affection, friendship, and insight. We can find moments free of ego, agenda, posturing. Some of these moments transform lives. All of them offer the opportunity for a new perception.

Michael W. Fox, vice president of the Humane Society of the United States, has written numerous books and articles about respectful and loving communion among humans, animals, and nature. One afternoon when I was speaking to Michael about the family of animals that had come to live on my small farm, some in rather unusual fashion as strays and gifts, he said, "Ah yes, they will all become your familiars." A "familiar" is defined as "an attendant spirit, often taking animal form." The many creatures who share the farm with my family are not with us just as pets, livestock, exhibits, predators, prey, or vermin—but as familiars. They have become our teachers, companions, and confidants, and their company adds an indescribable richness to our lives.

Animals offer tremendous help by simply being who and

what they are. They are beings who still remember the original instructions given them by an ancient universe. Storyteller Joseph Bruchac speculates that perhaps animals are wiser than human beings because they do not forget how to behave: "A bear never forgets it is a bear, yet human beings often forget what a human must do. Humans forget to take care of their families and forget to show respect to other things. They become confused because of material possessions and power."

As we observe the lives of the many creatures who live with and around us, what unfolds is an array of opportunities to learn about ourselves and our world, to grasp life's paradoxes, ironies, and mysteries that surround and often confuse us. The messages can be as formidable and dramatic as animal imagery that aids us in healing from disease, or as subtle and ordinary as a sleeping cat in the sun who offers the gentle reminder to "slow down, relax, enjoy life."

Although the animals in my life have long been providing me with insight and inspiration, one particular animal companion led me to acknowledge the impact of animals upon my life and work. Keesha, a Shepherd-Malamute mix, was the first animal in my life to insist that I engage her not as owner or master, but as partner and friend. And it was her story that started me on the path to this book.

Keesha was my friend, my confidant, my angel and, ultimately, my teacher. I first began writing about Keesha and her powerful healing lessons while I was recuperating from radiation treatments for aggressive, metastatic neck cancer. Only thirty-seven when I was initially diagnosed with a malignant tumor in my mouth, my medical prognosis was poor. These tumors are usually found in old, cigar-smoking, heavy-drinking men. When they appear in young, clean-living women like me, they usually spread like a chemical fire. When the tumor advanced to my lymph nodes in 1988, my doctors didn't expect me to survive another two years.

Like so many of us who have lived the suburban, civilized life, I'd always been shielded from sickness and death (which I have since learned is no blessing), and I knew little about how to live with a serious illness, much less how to die from one. According to my doctors, there was no reason to believe that I wouldn't be dying, and soon.

A friend has a phrase for those who have either faced their own death and survived, or who have experienced the death of a loved one. He calls them "the Initiated." The words, "You have cancer," launched my initiation. A sickening riot of feelings cemented my new-found status as initiate: Terror, hysteria, retching fear—these words described me on my good days. Because no one in my family or circle of friends had ever faced a serious or terminal illness, they could offer no counsel aside from their own terror at watching a relatively young woman face a grim prognosis. Where was I to find examples of how to live what was left of my life? Where does an initiate go for help? Finding no answers among anyone I knew, I turned to the only hopeful memory I had: Keesha.

In 1981, Keesha had died of cancer. Her disease started exactly where mine had, in the mouth. Her symptoms were the same as mine, including problems with eating and swallowing. Keesha's treatments were the same, too: weeks of daily radiation. Keesha eventually died of her disease, but she lived with remarkable zest and exuberance until the end. Suddenly, years after her death, Keesha and I were together once again, this time in the spirit of similar circumstance, and I felt a renewed bond with her. In my memories of Keesha, I would find the help I was seeking.

During the year-long course of my surgeries, metastases,

Keesha   PHOTO: SUSAN McELROY

and treatments it was Keehsa's example I chose to follow. When I was in the first stages of cancer what I valued most were my memories of Keesha's complete and graceful acceptance of every part of her illness and debilitation. One incident in particular had a profound impact on me, and even more so years later. Several weeks before her death, Keesha had become quite weak from her disease. The long daily strolls along the marsh near our home became shorter and slower as her cancer spread. In her healthier days, Keesha's greatest joy had been to swim in the deep lagoons filled with cattails and marsh grass. But now, too frail to swim, she looked to the glossy, shallow pools of rain that peppered our streets. At every opportunity, Keesha would plop into a big puddle and splash and bark for as long as I'd let her. The look on her face during those times was the look of a hog in a wallow. On our last excursion together she was only days away from death, yet she was in bliss.

From a dog splashing in a rain puddle, I learned about choice. Regardless of how much time I had left, I could choose to celebrate whatever possibilities life had to offer me each moment. Or, I could curl up and die. We, the Initiated, can be possessed by a manic sense of urgency and dread unknown to most people. It is a curse and a blessing. The urgency keeps your priorities straight, but it can paralyze momentum and cripple one's best efforts with fear. The antidote to that fear is to practice joy in the moment. I learned that the choice between celebration or dread is mine. Keesha's lesson is still with me today and has changed how I am in the world. At joy, Keesha was a master.

Through Keesha's inspiration, I somehow kept my humor, most of my friends, and my activities while undergoing cancer treatment. It would be a kindly understatement to say I had been dragged kicking and whining through the previous three-plus decades of my life. Always believing that life owed me something, I would complain bitterly when I didn't get what I thought I deserved. Sarcasm and rebelliousness were my most characteristic coping tools, and fear about anything and everything was my prime motivator. By the time I was faced with cancer, I was a sick, scared little girl. I truly believe that Keesha and cancer matured and healed me.

Most of the stories submitted for this book are heartfelt tributes to the lives of much-beloved animals who lived with their human companions for many years, accompanying them through failed marriages, lost jobs, deaths of loved ones and friends, and countless other major life passages. These strong ties between people and their animal companions were often the only enduring, secure bond to sustain them through difficult times. For most people, a relationship with a domestic animal is the only link they have with the animal nations. Thankfully, it is a powerful one. Keith Smith acknowledges this connection in *Mourning Sickness*, a book that chronicles his grieving and healing process after the loss of his young wife to cancer.

Your pet can help pull your attention away from you and your pain, and petting a soft creature who loves and depends on you reduces stress enormously. My little attention grabber and stress reliever is named Trevi after the famous fountain in

Rome. She was named after a fountain because for the first two months she was around, she peed on all my worldly possessions. Trevi is a "Zen Beagle"—all material things are equal in her eyes. These creatures listen to ancient voices that are only whispers to us. Their instinct to survive and exist in the moment, to fully attend to the sights, scents, and sounds that surround, speak to an old way of being.

When I cried in Trevi's presence she has licked my tears, looked up at me as if to say, "Wouldn't you rather play?" I would, I do.

Ted Andrews, author of *Animal-Speak*, suggests, "Every animal is a gateway to the phenomenal world of the human spirit. What most fail to realize is that what they think of animals reflects the way they think of themselves." The more I consider this principle, the more I see it at work every day in my own life. For instance, I get frustrated by animals who are standoffish and not free with their affection. I also realize that this, not coincidentally, is the aspect that I most dislike in myself, especially when I exhibit it in my family. My animals are extraordinarily adept at reflecting the stuck places in my life and serving them up to the cold light of personal scrutiny. Veterinarian and writer Judith Rae Swanson agrees.

My new dog, Lulu, would bite when she felt threatened. A male friend of mine grabbed her once to pick her up and she bit his hand. He said, "Typical woman, bites without warning!" I replied, "Typical man, grabs without permission!" Now Lulu no longer bites, but she has taught me to stand up for my rights.

Our pets are also exceptional judges of character, and the way we treat our pets is an unfailing indication of our own character as well. Animal consultant Judee Curcio-Wolfe was once told by her grandfather, "If you want to know how someone is going to treat you, just watch how they treat your animals when they think no one is looking." Judee remembered the merit of his advice when she found herself in the midst of an abusive relationship. In addition to recognizing the personal problems with her partner, she realized that this man had never gotten along peacefully with her horses. He was often short-tempered with them and they acted anxiously around him much of the time. In addition, he teased Judee for her ideas about animal communication and for her deep love of animals. Eventually, Judee left the relationship and promised herself she wouldn't make the same mistake again. When the time came to consider a new partner, Judee decided that she would not commit herself to someone who mocked her, and who couldn't or wouldn't share her affinity for animals. She also decided that the selection process would include input from her horses, Star and Tia.

Judee met a new man, Jeff, and eventually brought him home to meet her horses. The signs were encouraging. Jeff is a tall, big-boned man, but her two red Arabians showed no fear of him. They both came up to sniff and nuzzle his wonderful red hair. Judee said she knew Star was telling her, "Well, his hair is the right color. . . ." But the true test for Judee came one evening when Jeff went out alone to feed and water the horses. Judee walked out to the barn a bit later to do some chores and suddenly heard raucous laughter coming from one of the horse stalls. She peeked inside, and there stood Jeff and Star by the water bucket. Star was sticking his nose in and out of the jet of water pouring from the faucet, spraying water everywhere and saturating them both. While Judee watched unseen and delighted, she recalled her grandfather's message. In that moment, Judee knew she could trust Jeff to treat her with the same gentleness and humor that he so generously bestowed upon her best friend, Star. Today, Judee and Jeff are happily married with Star's and Tia's blessing, of course.

O ur companion animals can teach us how to open up to love again after a painful loss. For me, the death of Keesha was so extraordinary a loss that I quickly bestowed upon her the status of canine sainthood. For many years after her death, I found good reasons why I couldn't get another dog: too busy, never home enough, too many roommates, hard to find places to live, too expensive ... the list was painfully endless. Yet during these years I dreamed of the new dog I would bring into my life. Then I got cancer. My dreams of puppies faded before the all-encompassing challenge of the disease. Instead, I dreamed of angels hovering over me, and of huge black radiation machines aimed at my head. It wasn't until the reality of a new marriage and a new home six years later that my puppy dreams returned.

"Arrow" was the name I chose for my new dog before I ever saw her. Just like the song, it would be "Me and my Arrow, wherever we go, it's me and my Arrow." I fantasized that Arrow would be part Collie, part Shepherd, brown and fuzzy.

Somehow, I believed she would find me, and she did. I found her at a dog pound: a Shepherd-Collie mix, brown and fuzzy. Abandoned along with four litter mates on a commercial fishing dock, she was skin and bones and stank of rotten fish. But there was my dog Arrow, and I recognized her instantly.

When I brought her home, the rest of the story was supposed to go something like, "and we lived happily ever after." But it wasn't that way at all. Arrow is a jewel but Keesha and her gifts were diamonds, and I missed the diamonds. Overwhelmed with feelings of disappointment brought about by my constant comparisons between Arrow and Keesha, I blamed Arrow for not being the puppy I had wanted her to be. I rationalized that Arrow had serious personality faults. In fact, her only "fault" was that she wasn't Keesha.

One night in mid-winter, a subtle but miraculous shift occurred and all the frustration and upset between Arrow and me dissolved in an instant. I was looking at old photos of Keesha. Suddenly, I thought I was seeing pictures of Arrow. The feeling was so uncanny, so dreamlike, that I shook my head to clear it and stared again at the photos. Inexplicably, in that instant, Arrow and Keesha had somehow become one. That is, the love had become one.

Arrow's loyalty had sustained us until that moment. My feelings for Arrow had been conditional, even absent at times, but her devotion never wavered. She trusted that I would find my way to her, just as she had somehow found her way to me. Now, I can't imagine ever loving another dog the way I love her. Another dog owner, Fran Haas, expressed similar feelings after the passing of her much beloved dog, Dixie:

I no longer rage against God for depriving me of Dixie's love because I understand that God used her to teach me what love truly is. Despite all the odds against it, I love my new dog, Beamer, as much as I loved Dixie. I could never have been capable of genuine, sincere, unconditional love without loving Dixie first. All I have learned about loving dogs was taught to me by Dixie. What an exquisite silver lining to discover!

Countless people have said to me, somewhat apologetically, that they treat their pets as if they were their children. These words are never said in a proud or even matter-of-fact manner, but rather as if there is something sordid about treating a pet like a child. To the contrary, animal companions are a wonderful repository for love. Sometimes, they are the only beings available to receive and return affection and nurturing. My friend Maureen Mason wrote about her new puppy, Molly, in a story she called, "My Daughter Molly." Although I have known Maureen for more than a decade, it wasn't until I received her letter that I learned her childlessness wasn't of her choosing. She writes:

> When people ask if I have children, I answer both yes and no. "I have three dogs," I say. But I must confess that they are my children—the ones I couldn't have—especially Molly. My husband and I spent years trying to have children, altering our lives as we tried this route and that, submitting to test after test. As we were in the throes of trying, the major problem that prevented us from conceiving went undetected. Although I didn't know it, I was becoming more ill with each passing month until one Janu-

ary day I was overcome with abdominal pain that never left. In the end, the only option was a hysterectomy. . . .

As I recuperated from surgery, I longed to nurture the daughter or son I would never have. All of life around me, whether it was children playing in the street or diaper commercials on television, was a constant reminder of the child I would never have. My need to cuddle someone soft who was in need of a mother was overwhelming. And so we brought home a new puppy—our third dog. She was a blue merle Sheltie with a mottled face and one brown eye and one blue eye. As soon as I saw her I fell in love with her. The name Molly came to mind and suited her so well, we named her instantly. Although I was only in my ninth week of recuperation from surgery, and still moving very slowly, I rejoiced in cuddling my warm, furry baby, having her sleep in my arms, playing with her, teaching her, guiding her—but mostly just loving her. We have gone to several obedience classes and because of all the time we have spent together, it is she—now as a young adult dog—who follows me around the house and lies next to me so closely that I can feel the warmth of her body.

Molly is not human. I know that. And I'm well aware of the difference. But Molly is my little girl, the girl who now looks up at me as she lays atop my foot, as I write about the daughter I did have.

Rachael Naomi Remen, M.D., offers workshops for patients and physicians to explore the many realms of healing. Teaching at a yoga retreat for cancer patients, Naomi spoke of a powerful process that celebrates thanksgiving, which she believes is a core element of the healing process. The actual task is simple. Workshop participants are asked to give thanks for what they have. The event can take hours as those giving thanks become graphically aware, some for the first time, of the bounty in their universe. "I give thanks for my bed, for my blue sheets, for hot water, for plumbing," they chant. "For my red shoes, my black shoes, my tennis shoes, my dishwasher, the roof over my head, the food on my table . . . for life, for my family, my car, paper and pens, cheesecake . . ." and on and on into the night.

Realizing and acknowledging the many gifts in our lives can be a powerful tool of personal transformation and of healing. My animal companions remind me daily of the joy in simple things, and to give thanks to the universe for the unending bounty in my life. As I was working on this chapter, the first hot days of Oregon summer finally, thankfully, arrived. In the thick heat of one afternoon, I watched my chicken "family" gathered around their favorite dusting hole. One hen was stretched out in the dust bowl, splashing herself with a cloud of fine dirt and clucking in blissful, low tones. Several other chickens nestled nearby, chortling to each other and stretching their wings out in the sun. Two hours later, they were still lounging. Thank you, I thought, for dirt, and for the glory of warm summer afternoons that are so treasured here in the Northwest. And thank you for the chickens who remind me to slow down and soak up the simple joy of a sunny day.

Many people wrote letters about the simple, yet far-reaching gifts their pets gave them over a lifetime. Nowhere have I seen the joy of simple gifts and of thanksgiving more poignantly demonstrated than in the following story by Susan Huskins.

We lived in a large house and my cat, Sammi, always took pride in leaving me small field mice at the door each morning. She was extremely proud of these successful hunting ventures and looked forward to my praise of these small gifts at the door. Then, we had to move to a very small apartment. There were no fields for her to play in, and only a few trees to climb.

When I finally let her out solo, she greeted me at the door the following morning as was her habit, talking up a storm and just as proud as she could be. When I looked down, there at my feet were two small pine cones. I was absolutely amazed. She continued to bring a pine cone or two to the door each morning until the day she died.

I will never forget Sammi. My little cat showed me that no matter what the situation, we can find a way to make the best of it. To this day, when things are hard to deal with, I see her at the door with those pine cones.

Many stories I received were from or about children and spoke of the especially close relationships children have with their pets. Children are unencumbered by the often rigid notions we adults harbor about animals and their roles in the world. When you combine the innocence, imagination, unconditional love, and flair for adventure that animals and children possess in abundance, the opportunities for growth, insight, and healing are amazing and inimitable. Animals can lead children willingly and enthusiastically to new levels of growth, wisdom, and maturity. Shannon Yoder, a fifteen-year-old, wrote about her experiences volunteering in a program for handicapped horseback riders. The insights she shares have come to her through her love and passion for horses, yet what she has learned encompasses far more than horse care.

I started volunteering at Thorncroft Therapeutic Horseback Riding, Inc., because it was a good way to get service hours. Horses were involved and I needed a project for my Girl Scout Gold Award. I knew I would be working with disabled people, but I did not think much about that aspect of the program.

Before I started working at Thorncroft, I felt very uncomfortable around disabled people. I didn't know how to act or how to have a conversation with them. But the more I volunteered, the more I began to enjoy the people and the work and I have learned a great deal about different conditions of disability. One rider, John, has trouble walking. He has a hard time trying to do anything with his right arm and his speech is not that clear, but he can ride horses. He can groom them and tack them up. He also competes in horse shows. The horse has the legs, John has the willpower. Together they can do almost anything!

I see things happen that some people never thought possible. When a patient sits up for the first time, takes his first step, or begins to steer a horse on her own, I feel like I helped make these moments happen. These accomplishments that may seem so little in other people's eyes are so big to me. The best moment is to see a patient smile. That smile says, "Look at me! I can do it!" And I can't help but smile with them.

Children grappling with difficult trauma or life-threatening illness often withdraw from the world searching for a safe and healing place. Sometimes an animal, just by its mere presence, can be the source of safety and healing for a child in despair. Perhaps this is because animals listen without judgment or advice, and demonstrate peaceful acceptance and love in the moment. Robin Kovary works in a pet-assisted therapy program. She shared the following story:

Shiva was an exceptionally sweet, affectionate, and well-behaved female Bull Mastiff. We worked together for many years. I'll never forget one visit in particular that involved a special little girl. Shiva and I had already been volunteering for several months in the pediatrics division of a large New York hospital. Many of the children there had serious, life-threatening diseases. Each month, Shiva and I visited this hospital together, hoping to give these young patients a way to get their minds off their worries and pain for at least a little while. The children who were ambulatory were allowed to walk Shiva through the halls of the hospital. They loved the smiles and attention they received from the doctors and nurses who passed them. Other children would brush Shiva's brindle coat, pet her soft ears, or have their photographs taken with her.

There was one child, however, who never once spoke, interacted, or showed us anything but the saddest of facial expressions during our visits. She was about six-years old, very thin, and had no hair left because of her extensive chemo-therapy treatments. I was told that she was in the advanced

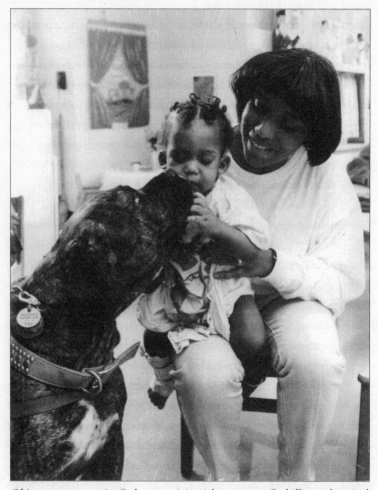

Shiva on a pet-assisted therapy visit with a mom and child at a hospital.
PHOTO: BRAD HESS

stages of cancer and that she was both physically and emotionally depressed. The staff told me that she rarely spoke to anyone
anymore, not even to her caregivers at the hospital, despite their
best efforts to draw her out.

Around the fourth month into our pet therapy visits, Shiva
herself was diagnosed with cancer and had to undergo extensive
surgery. She was unable to visit the children for more than a
month. When Shiva was fully recovered, we resumed our visits.
The children wanted to know why we hadn't come the month
before. I explained that Shiva had cancer, that she had to have
surgery, and that she needed time to heal before she was able to
come back and visit them. Well, suddenly the little girl with no
hair lit up! For the first time in all those months, she flooded us
with questions: Was Shiva going to lose her hair? Was she going
to die?

The staff members were amazed. More than a dozen hospi-
talized children in the room became more animated, full of
curiosity about the dog who shared their illness. And I was told
afterward by a nurse that Shiva's visit was enormously helpful
in allowing them to reach the seemingly unreachable little girl.
Less than one year later, Shiva died of a ruptured heart-based
tumor. Shiva's registered name, given to her as a puppy, was
"Guardian Angel." She certainly lived up to it.

The relationship between children and animals can be so therapeutic that programs exist specifically to bring troubled children together with animals. One of the premiere national
programs of this sort is Green Chimneys, a residential treatment center, housed on more than one hundred acres of

PHOTO: JODI FREDIANI

rolling farmland in upstate New York. At any given time, about 102 inner-city youngsters share the campus with more than 150 animals, including companion animals, farm animals, and wildlife. "Many of the Green Chimneys children arrive with histories of neglect or abuse," explains Dr. Samuel Ross, Jr. of Green Chimneys residential program. "Many are also learning disabled and have never experienced success at school. They have had a rocky existence at home, in school, and in the community. They become defeated because they have failed in those things by which children get judged. At Green Chimneys, children soon learn that there has never been an animal who asked a child his or her achievement test score." When these children write poems and stories, or draw pictures, they describe a treasured communion.

> The animals never yell at me.
> The animals never make me do things
> I don't want to do.
> They don't expect too much of me.
> They don't get mean or mad.
> They're always there to run with me.
> And make me feel not sad.
>
> —*Michael, age 10*
> GREEN CHIMNEYS

For children who have experienced the world as a hurtful, unsafe place, an animal may be the only teacher the children can relate to and trust. The following letters were sent to me from several members of a high-school stress-reduction group. Each writer touted the unique value of her animal companion as a formidable stress-buster.

My dog Murphy listens to me with an animated face and when I get home, he is always in a good mood and happy to see me. Murphy helps me feel better about "me." When my problems depress me, Murphy's soft touch and comforting manner are very reassuring. Because he doesn't talk back, I can tell him my private thoughts and I know he won't share them with others. Another thing we do is play catch: I will throw the ball and he will fetch until we are both tired. This game makes me feel less stressed and more childlike. Playing with Murphy helps me to sleep better at night.

—Melissa Bean

I had mononucleosis for two years and was bedridden for half of that. During that time, I didn't have any support from family or friends. All I had was a very special cat, Pepper. I went into a depression and did not have very good feelings about myself. Pepper would curl up on me and comfort me with her purring. She was always there to listen to my problems and at times it seemed as though she would subconsciously give me advice on what to do. Animals definitely help me deal with stress. I can tell them anything and they won't tell anyone else.

—Trina Field

Bootsi is my nine-month-old kitten. She's my best friend and I could never give her up. When I come home from school, she's the only one excited to see me, and she cries for me to pick her up. She always knows if I am sad or not. Whenever I need someone to talk to, she's right there to listen to me. I love my cat and don't know what I'd do without her.

— Heather Parkinson

In a passage from *Animals: Our Return to Wholeness* by Penelope Smith, I found myself face-to-face with a more global and exhilarating way to view my activities here on earth. Suppose we humans truly believed that every action we took affected the entire world in some manner. What if a butterfly flapping its wings in Paris could somehow affect the weather in New York? I first read of this intriguing idea of the interconnectedness of all things in Fritjof Capra's book, *Uncommon Wisdom*, which explores the new paradigms of interconnectedness in quantum physics and in many other sciences. Animals may, in some indescribable fashion, already embrace this global communion that we have yet to acknowledge fully. In her book, Penelope writes about her chorus of roosters.

> As they crowed in a series of rounds with each other, I became aware of a magnetism around them stretching out to the sky . . . I connected with all the roosters around the planet and I knew, at that moment, that they were responsible for bringing up the sun. I realized that many folk tales were true about animals' different functions, no matter how bizarre it seemed to our Western analytical mode of thinking. I knew totally that without the roosters crowing, the sun would not rise. It was their duty, and that's why they started a few hours beforehand, to prime the sky and . . . the earth to prepare for the sun's appearance.

In many cases, as I was writing about a particular concept or idea for this book, I would receive a letter that expanded my idea to the next level, or put a twist on a concept that I hadn't ever considered. Such was the case when I was writing about the interconnectedness of all things. Sharon Callahan, who operates a unique animal healing program in Shasta, California, proposes that animals may reflect far more than what is happening in their immediate environment.

> Animals have not lost their profound attunement to Earth as a living being, and remain intimately aware of planetary fluctuations. They sense earth changes both locally and on all parts of the globe. Because they perceive holographically, they are keenly aware of the suffering of other members of their particular species, as well as that of the collective animal soul. As the great cats are driven to extinction in ever increasing numbers, is it any wonder that your cat suffers from nonspecific anxiety? As the wolf continues to be persecuted in Alaska and other areas, is it any wonder that your dog manifests neurotic behavior at times?

Carl Jung speaks of our collective unconscious—the part of us that is shared across race, gender, and cultures. Perhaps humans share the fear, pain, and suffering of the collective human soul, regardless of where we live or who we know. And perhaps animals share the psychic burdens of their own animal families.

▲ ▲ ▲

The Best Mouser on the Farm

I learned perseverance through adversity from a black kitten with the feline equivalent of cerebral palsy. Toot couldn't move in a straight line to save his soul, but he was the best mouser we had on the farm. We were never sure if the mouse was so confused by Toot's gyrations it couldn't move, or if it laughed itself to death watching Toot approach.

We credit Toot with helping one of our friends start on the road to recovery from alcoholism. Living out in the country as we did, we were rather particular who came on our property to hunt. Of the friends we allowed to hunt, one was an alcoholic. One morning this hunter, after taking more than a few good swigs of whiskey out of a bottle stashed in his car, headed off with his rifle in search of some moving targets. On his way into our pastures, he suddenly stopped and stared into our corn crib for several long moments. Then, he abruptly turned around, went back to his car, and put his rifle away. He slowly tottered up to the house, drunk and visibly shaken, and asked if he could have a cup of coffee. He drank it without saying a word. He appeared to be in shock. Fearing that something horrible was in the corn crib, Mom went out to check. When she returned from the building, it was obvious to us that she was trying very hard to hold her laughter. The hunter left after two more cups of coffee, and Mom finally told us what she'd seen.

The hunter must have seen Toot hunting in the crib.

Although Toot's handicap had become quite unnoticeable to us, we're sure the hunter must have thought he was hallucinating. And we never bothered to enlighten him. To our knowledge, the hunter never drank alcohol again after that day. Toot had saved the life of a friend.

—Debbie Sorenson

Leaving the Fast Lane

Life in the fast lane held less and less appeal for me by the time I was forty-five, but for some reason I kept it up, day in, day out. Working nights and long hours as a professional chef in Las Vegas led me into an every-evening wildness that would scare even a hardened drinker, which I was. My drinking had become so severe that it finally plunged me into a lonely living terror only a true alcoholic can understand. By the fall of 1991, I had even spent time in a local hospital because of the side-effects from my drinking disease. But I was quickly released, and would soon meet a friend who would change my life completely.

The day my world changed, I was watching the World Series. Drinking helped me to urge on my team. My roommate and his girlfriend came in and told me they had spotted a stray dog at the local convenience store. I'm not quite sure how it happened, but by that evening the dusty-colored, scruffy little dog was fed and resting on the couch in my apartment. He looked like he'd never had a bath or a grooming and I was reluctant even to keep him around. But my roommate piped up, "Can't you just picture him with some eleven-year-old boy, just the two of them knockin' around together?" Somehow, I couldn't get his words out of my head.

A few years before during a physical exam, I had told a doctor about my drinking problem. He told me that I was in the grips of a very serious disease and that there was little he

Larry and Homer with Larry's three-year A.A. sobriety chip on his collar.

could do to help me. He suggested that I find myself a steady girlfriend and change my lifestyle. If I couldn't find a girlfriend, he told me I should find a dog. "What for?!" I asked in surprised ignorance. The doctor said I needed someone or something that needed me.

He must have been right. After "Homer" came into my life, I tried hard to keep up my old habits of drinking and coming home at odd hours, but knowing that Homer was home alone was just too much for me to bear. I started heading home earlier and earlier each night. Homer was so glad to see me! All that affection had an effect on me that was just like magic. Instead of drinking my after-work hours away, Homer and I began wandering through the parks and church parking lots nearby. I made an attempt to find out where Homer came from, but the convenience store owner said that Homer had been abandoned there by transients, so it appeared that the little dog was mine from now on. A visit to the vet and the groomer, plus a new rubber ball, gave Homer a sense of belonging and I took him along with me everywhere. We were seldom apart, and he remains a favorite guest everywhere we go. During a trip to Arizona to visit my daughters, I missed Homer so much that my drinking problem suddenly worsened. At that point, however, I was finally ready for help. My girls called an old friend of mine who introduced me to Alcoholics Anonymous (A.A.), and the program worked wonders for me. But I remain firmly convinced that A.A. was not fully responsible for my recovery. A giant piece of my success had found its way into my heart many months before: my Homer dog. Since Homer and I have become companions I see a different world than before, a world filled with possibilities, hope, and change. Homer brought something important to my life. Through my love for him and his unconditional love for me, change became possible. Maybe Homer brought me back a piece of the youth I had lost in Southeast Asia or the trust that I had lost at the end of my marriage. What it comes down to is that I now have faith in a power greater than myself.

In the photo of Homer and me, you'll notice that my A.A. three-year sobriety medal is around Homer's neck, not mine.

—*Larry Chamberlain*

Oh wisdom
in your fur coat
and whiskers.
What don't you know?
sometimes I believe
I have seen my soul searched
in your eyes,
how much time passes
between us without word?
how much do you know
that I've just begun
to understand?

spirit of grace
and humor
on all fours.

—Pam Reinke

There is one who is not free.
She gave herself the life of a
servant or is it a sister?
Who out of love needs no one else but me.

She has stood between horn and hoof.
She has bled for me, cried, sung and played.

Once I asked her to bite a drunk who angered me.
But she, in wisdom, would not.
Yet when I was alone and afraid of someone,
She was unafraid and stood up between us
crying, "No!
No!"

You have followed me for a long while.
I hope when this is over you follow me to the spirit place
spirit home
spirit woman
spirit hound.

— Teresa Martino
LEARNING FROM EAGLE,
LIVING WITH COYOTE

Living in Vertical Time

The Teachings of Murray the "Buru"

The First Church of the Disciples of Murray is not some new cult, even though Murray, its spiritual leader, is a jackass—a real one with big hairy ears and a bray that can bring down a barn. Murray lives in the pasture right behind my house. I established a small church in his name because Murray is so special. Why, you ask? Because Murray is an ass of great character, and as a screenwriter, I can tell you, character is everything! Murray is the embodiment of humility, patience, and tolerance. He never complains, even when some fool throws a board into the pasture with nails in it and Murray steps on one and can barely walk for weeks. He suffers the bullying abuse of Julio, his llama pasture mate, with a calm demeanor, moving just far enough away to bring it to a halt. He is exceedingly present. When he is with me , I feel that I am with someone. His presence is calm and centering. With him, I feel the whirring insanity of my mind decelerate. He teaches me to stand, to be, to breathe, to take my place on the planet with pride and dignity—in this very moment.

We must all suffer the obnoxious llamas of life. We all stand in the rain of collective ignorance, pelted by the media. We all find our lives constrained by the barbed wire of our own minds. I, for one, someday hope to conduct myself with the centered peacefulness of Murray. That is why he is so special to me. That is why he is my living teacher—my "buru."

Murray lives in vertical time. I've been there a few times.

To some extent or another, we all experience vertical time. But most of us live much of our lives in horizontal time: a plane upon which our lives are stretched out like railroad tracks running across the Great Plains. The tracks begin somewhere and continue until they reach those big bumper things you find at the end of tracks in railroad yards: For our purposes here, we'll call that death.

Most of the time I walk this track, stepping from tie to tie. As I walk along, I often stop to look back and remember "events," things that "happened to me." These events serve to fuel my paranoia when I again face my future, projecting these memories onto other imagined events to come. Murray doesn't

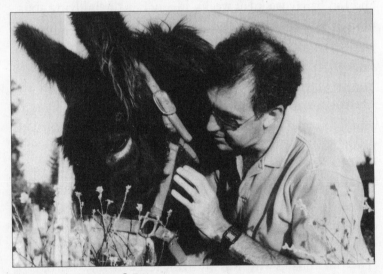

Murray the Buru and Brian   PHOTO: KYLE KOEPPEN

do this. No animal does it the same way we hairless monkeys do, but Murray has a distinct Buddha-like quality about him.

I wonder what Murray gets from me, besides carrots. Love is an obvious answer but I'm not sure it suffices. I think presence is a better word. When I'm with Murray, I move closer to vertical time: I'm much more contented just to be. I am temporarily satisfied. I don't need money or things or success or sex or assurances. I have contentment. This is it. The more I enter this state, I have a feeling that it feeds something back to Murray. Sharing deepens the richness of the moment. Spiritual leader Meher Baba said, "Things that are real are given and received in silence." Something real goes on between Murray and me in silent, vertical time.

Imagine, for a moment, that Murray could talk. I would venture to guess that he would not be capable of lying. To lie you have to have an eye firmly fixed on the past because all your energy is tied up in suppressing facts that linger there. Lying happens in horizontal time, and Murray doesn't live there.

I went to a talk given years ago by Reverend William Sloan Coffin. He started his talk with seven words that still echo inside me. He said, "The function of government is to lie." He continued, "Lies require violence to support them . . . and violence requires lies to support it." There it was, a graduate course in political and ethical science in twenty words. I think if Murray could speak, he would say things like that.

—*Brian Narelle*
CREATION SPIRITUALITY
(Jan/Feb 1993)

Tristan

A Being of Great Mystery

His name was Tristan. His zest for life was indomitable. His soul was magnanimous and I frankly don't think he ever knew how small his body was. Entering a room, he would fill it by his presence. When he was fourteen years old he was attacked by a Pitbull. The veterinarian who treated him said of Tristan: "Any other dog his age and size would have died. He had an immense spirit to live." That was Tristan.

My getting to know Tristan was a gradual affair; indeed, I am still learning things about him months after his death. He was a being of great mystery who kept his secrets and mysteries well guarded. Who will ever know the secrets behind the eyes—and into the souls—of animals? When the mystics tell us that "the soul is not in the body, but the body in the soul," I realize that this does not apply merely to humans but to animals as well.

When Tristan was just a few years old I took him to visit a friend in a nearby town. When he had been in her house only a short time, she said, "My, Tristan is a beautiful person." I said, "Come again. What did you say?" She repeated her phrase, "Tristan is a beautiful person." I told her that I had felt for some time that he was indeed a person, but was struck that she used that term so deliberately. "Oh," she said matter-of-factly, "some dogs are dogs and some are persons. It was absolutely clear after just a few minutes of his being in this house that Tristan is a person."

Today I would go one step further in my understanding of this person who was my dog. I would say that he was also a spirit. He was certainly my spirit-guide for seventeen years, and after his death he has appeared in dreams among a pantheon of spirits that have assisted me over the years. What realms did he come from? What realms did he know? What realms did he return to? That is where his dignity and ability to keep his own counsel and his own secrets take over. Living with an animal like him reinforces one's capacity for living in mystery and letting mystery be mystery.

There were uncanny things that Tristan knew and did. He would participate in his own fashion at meetings I would have in our home. Tristan would invariably greet each visitor in his way and would then plunk himself in the middle of the room, sleeping or feigning sleep during our deliberations. His presence was real; his participation was his own. I was often struck by how keenly he listened to human conversations. Our neighbors had a female dog named Lady who was Tristan's friend. Once several of us were having a conversation and the generic noun "lady" was mentioned by someone. Tristan went wild. He ran all over the house barking and jumping. He had been listening so intently to us that he found the one word in our conversation that applied to his world and responded appropriately. This one incident alerted me to how, ears up and pointed in any one of thirty-three possible directions, this animal was a keen listener. We ought to watch our conversations around animals.

Tristan was an amazing judge of character. Once I was

having work done on our house by a friend who was a car-
penter. He brought a buddy with him to assist him in doing
the job. But for the many weeks it took to complete the work,
Tristan never let this friend's buddy pet him. He always
growled under his breath when this fellow came near him.
Months after the job was completed my friend learned that his
buddy had skipped town with the money I had paid them for
the work. How do animals know such things? After that, I
always made a point of Tristan greeting every worker I ever
hired in the house.

Tristan loved to make up games and get people to play
them. For example, he would get two or three of us out into the
backyard and would run in a circle, faster and faster and suddenly jump in the air and turn around in the other direction,
daring us to catch him. We never did. Not one person; not two;
not three. But he always created the circle just large enough to
give us a fighting chance—and keep us in the game. It always struck me that his purpose in game playing was not to
"win"—whatever that means—but to have a go at it, to have a
good time.

Tristan was my spiritual director in so many ways. He kept
my life and work in perspective and was a companion in
writing twelve of the fourteen books I have written. When I
wrote books before I had a computer, I would put papers from
the typewriter and from my notes on the floor around my
desk. Tristan would, after a few hours of being with me in my
work, get up and deliberately walk on my stacks of papers. I
felt he was reminding me that, as exciting as ideas can be, life

contains other realities as well. It was time for a walk in the woods, time for leaving the work of the mind behind. And walk we would with him leading the way, turning back to see if I was coming along and not dragging my feet, and surging on ahead sniffing, smelling, chasing, seeing, and hearing what my senses could only imagine was out there.

Walking a dog in the city always makes for conversation and communication with strangers. Little children will stop and ask to pet the dog and older people will stop to talk about the dog. Once when I was walking him on a street near our home a woman stopped and said, "Is that a Spitz?" I said yes. She said, "They have the best sense of humor of any dog." After Tristan died many people in the neighborhood stopped me when I was walking by myself to inquire about him; they missed him. Animals do that to people, especially people in a city. They become part of the spirit of a neighborhood.

During Tristan's last year, I took special pains to observe him ever more closely to try and learn what he was teaching me. At nights, he would spend most of his time at the far end of the bed pointing outward as if he were guarding me from any hostile spirits who might want to visit during the night. But invariably, almost nightly that last year, he would come up to my pillow and lay his head next to my head just for a brief time. Never more than five or ten minutes would our heads be next to each other. I miss that.

His last healthy day was special. He was ravenous and barked and barked at dinnertime. The next day at noon, I let him outside and soon after I saw him in our neighbor's yard, just standing there, not moving. I ushered him into our yard, and again he just stood there.

I took him to the vet. It was a tumor. The vet called me to say there was nothing they could do. "Then we should put him to sleep." I did not want him to suffer needlessly. She told me to come over right away, that they would ready him for that eventuality. When I arrived at the vet fifteen minutes later I was shocked to learn that Tristan had died. I had so wanted to hold him in my arms. I turned to my friend who had come to the vet hospital with me, "What does this mean? Why wasn't I with him when he died?" But the vet had the answer: "The two of you must have had an amazing communication between you," she said. "Because he died before I hung up the phone when talking to you. He died the exact moment you said we should put him to sleep. He was waiting for your permission to leave."

Rilke says: Somewhere there is/ an ancient enmity/ between our daily life/ and the great work.

With Tristan—and perhaps with all animals—there was no enmity between his daily life and the great work. There are lessons for me to learn from this. I will always be grateful to Tristan for his work and to the universe for lending me such a special co-worker. "All wisdom," Thomas Aquinas says, "is given to us on loan."

—*Matthew Fox*
CREATION SPIRITUALITY
(JAN/FEB 1993)

Grace

Twilight begins
The embrace of stars.
I attend to softening edges,
Watch the unassuming beauty of
Horses as they bow their heads
Over sweet, sun-dried grasses.

This is the most peaceful time I know.
Paced by clover-scented, rhythmic chewing,
Content with present abundance
I slow the natural pulse
Of earth and sky

To simple needs—
Warm breath on hand,
Comfortable intimacy in serene eyes.
For it is the horse's gift
To connect us with heaven
And our own footsteps.

Each evening
I look forward to this transition,
This precious mystery of
Communion with the still Earth
As I gently slip out of this binding human skin
And dance with child-like grace before the setting sun.

—Ronni Sweet

PHOTO: SUMNER W. FOWLER

CHAPTER TWO

Animals as Guardians and Guides

Men and women everywhere are being made acutely aware of the fact that something essential to life and well-being is flickering very low in the human species and threatening to go out entirely. This "something" has to do with such values as love ... unselfishness ... sincerity ... loyalty to one's best friend ... honesty ... enthusiasm ... humility ... goodness ... happiness ... fun. Practically every animal has these assets in abundance and is eager to share them, given the opportunity and the encouragement.

—JAY ALLEN BOONE
Kinship with All Life

Many of the letters and stories I received about animals who saved lives, guided careers, or steered people away from dangerous choices, referred to these special animals as "angels." Not surprisingly, when speaking of moments like these in our lives, many of us turn to spiritual terminology, the most readily accessible framework for expressing experiences and circumstances that are beyond our comprehension. For many, animals become angels and the mystical moments we share with animals seem to transcend the limits of our daily world.

Stories passed down through the ages proclaim that humans have been saved by the amazing grace of animal angels. We have been suckled by wolves, pulled drowning from the ocean by dolphins and whales, allowed a safe walk into the lion's den or the snake pit, and led to safety by mysteriously appearing animals who then vanish without a trace. I would include in this listing of animal angels and heroes those who gave up their bodies as heat or food for the lost and starving, as well as the animals who act as eyes, hands, and ears for those of us who depend upon their generous service.

We all hear about the dramatic stories that make the national news—dogs who rescue babies from burning buildings, cats that sound out a meow louder than a smoke alarm, the wolf who shelters shivering children lost in the wilderness. Those who have been rescued in this manner must feel especially blessed, touched by a gift of mercy from an unexpected being. A dramatic example of this special kind of sacrifice was sent to me by critical care nurse Debbie Sorenson:

In my profession, I have heard of stories of animals who sacrifice themselves to save the life of a human companion. One of the most memorable stories was of a German Shepherd covering a toddler with its body during a house fire. When the firefighters removed the dog's body, they were surprised to find the toddler still alive and suffering from only minor burns and smoke inhalation. The dog had been purchased to protect the family—it gave its life to do so.

What has always struck me most about these kinds of stories is not how they occurred, but that they occurred. There is enormous importance in the notion of another species voluntarily defending us, sometimes with its very life. We treasure these heroic animals and their uncompromising devotion. We offer them military medals and give them the ceremonial keys to our cities. Some animals are immortalized in books and statues, so moved are we at their great courage. Yet, ironically, humans who are willing to return the favor and sacrifice safety and perhaps even their lives for an animal—those who intercept the harpoon, the gun, and the club—are frequently perceived by society not as "angels" or Samaritans, but as lunatics or fanatics.

Whether we choose to view animals as angelic emissaries, as familiars, or simply as generous friends willing to help us out in time of need is a personal choice. What is most important is to choose a perspective and a language that allows you to absorb and express the magnanimity and mystery of another being electing, in one timeless moment or for a lifetime, to stand beside you as guardian or guide. Judee Curcio-Wolfe told me about a miraculous, life-saving moment that happened years ago between Judee and her dog. Judee practices a unique therapeutic form of touch or bodywork for animals, and is accomplished in nonverbal or intuitive communication with the animal. Judee has assisted many people in healing their relationships with their pets. By working on such problems as an animal's limp or a sudden, unusual fear or aggression, Judee might discover an old trauma or emotional issue for the animal and its owner. She focuses on opening her mind and heart to the animals brought to her for consultation and believes, as I do, that her mastery in intuiting the problems or frustrations of her animal clients is a skill we all have to varying degrees and can hone if we care to.

Anytime there was a challenge in my life it was an animal I went to for help and support. I grew up in a large family, and as a child, I always believed that I could talk to animals. And I believed that they talked back. I never stopped knowing that. I kept this treasured idea, this special "knowingness," close to me and shared it with few people. It seemed too precious a gift to speak of, as if in sharing it, I might diminish it somehow. When I began in my young twenties to talk to people about my ideas about animals and how we could speak with them, I was continually invalidated until I just stopped speaking about it.

Once when I was about ten, a puppy came to us almost frozen to death and I sensed that if we put him by the fire, he would warm up and be okay. No one else shared this belief, as the puppy was so cold he was almost rigid. But I wrapped him up in a warm blanket, and rubbed him all over and told him that he could come back to us, and that he didn't have to go. Instinctively, I worked on the puppy with much of the same bodywork techniques I still use today. Somehow inside, I simply knew that if I kept rubbing and massaging him, he would make it. It took two hours, during which time my family urged me to give it up because the puppy was dead, or nearly dead. But I just knew he was going to be okay. I knew that this dog was supposed to come back to be with me, and he did.

A few years later, I was spending the night at a girlfriend's house with another wonderful dog, Herman. I was twelve years old at the time and still cherished the belief that I could talk with animals. In fact, I had diligently practiced this kind of silent communication with Herman for quite some time. It was really windy that particular night, and we were sleeping in a tent out in my friend's huge backyard. At about two in the morning, Herman came running into the tent excited and upset. He woke me up, and I knew that he was saying, "Get out! Get out NOW!" Though silent, the intensity of the communication was so strong that I couldn't ignore it. I shook my girlfriend and told her we had to get out of the tent. I grabbed her arm and hauled her out. No sooner had we rushed out than a huge tree collapsed across the tent, smashing it. I stood there stunned and shaking. At first, I tried to tell myself that maybe I had imagined Herman's warning, but I knew that I couldn't invalidate what had happened between him and me. That wonderful little dog taught me so much about trusting myself and my abilities. Besides saving my life, he had given me the strength to follow my heart and honor my beliefs, regardless of the judgment and adversity that might come my way. Looking back, I believe now that most children know in their hearts what is true—it's fear that chases that knowingness away.

Ben Carson sent a story about his harrowing experience of being caught in a blizzard, and of the horses that guided him to safety.

The blizzard that struck Minnesota on Armistice Day in 1940 still brings shivers to the old timers who remember it. My dad was working on a neighboring farm a distance away, so Mom sent my brother and me to bring our herd of young heifers from a pasture about six miles from our farm. We put the bridles on Dollie and Dan, our team of strawberry-roan draft horses, and rode off into the storm. After considerable wandering over the trail, we arrived at the pasture gate. It was snowing so hard we could only see about thirty feet in any direction, so my brother went one way around the pasture, and I, on Dollie, went the other. The storm was increasing in fury, and it was impossible to determine any direction because of the thickness of the snow. I began to get the feeling that Dollie sensed what was going on and I finally laid the check rein on her neck, gave her head, and said, "Go find those cows, Dollie." Dollie moved ahead. I had not the foggiest notion where we were going when suddenly Dollie whinnied and out of a curtain of blowing snow came my brother, Arch, and the cows. The snow was so thick now that no landmarks were discernable and we lumbered along in a silence broken only by an infrequent exchange of our concerns about our fate. We had been trailing the herd for about an hour and had no idea if we were still in the pasture or had passed through without noticing. Arch and I were both worried, but knew of no better alternative than to let the horses have their heads and hope for the best.

Suddenly, we heard a voice shouting, "Over here!" It was Dad, standing in the open barn door. To this day, I am amazed at what those two horses did in a situation that must have required them to apply some long unused, inherited abilities. We were not aware of the danger we had faced until two days after the storm had passed. The news came over the radio that over twenty people had frozen to death during that blizzard.

Sometimes we need to be rescued from ourselves, our anger, our cruelty. Many stories I received told of companion animals who literally stepped between people arguing in an attempt to diffuse the situation. In a wonderful story by Jay Ellis Ransom, a big Collie serves as playground monitor for a class of rowdy boys, and "rescues" the youngsters from their fights and squabbling. Although the incident happened more than a half-century ago, the memory of it is still a vivid one for Jay.

In 1929, the entire year at Weatherwax High School passed without a single yard fight between us adolescent boys—a most unusual circumstance. As a junior that fall, I and my ebullient companions were accustomed to playful pummeling of one another's shoulder, alternately building up power blows until one or the other gave in. Occasionally, we'd get into real fisticuffs, but not that year.

We never determined where the huge, heavily coated Collie came from, or who owned him. But every morning before the first students arrived on the Weatherwax campus, the Collie began patrolling the school yard. And he stayed "on deck" until the last student had left the grounds.

Whenever a fight began, that Collie merely interposed his heavy body between the contestants so that neither youth could reach across him to the other. The Collie himself was too heavily built to be affected by any potential kicks against his sides. He never barked and he never bit. He just placed himself between the shouting combatants until they burst out laughing and quit trying to fight each other.

We found the dog's protectiveness especially amusing, and frequently put on a deliberate pounding just to get the Collie's attention. At best, we rarely got in more than a single punch before that all-seeing Collie had effectively separated us. Then we boys almost died laughing and if our laughing got too raucous, the big dog invariably separated us even further.

Rescue from emotional injury or abuse is no less stunning or heroic, yet rarely would these stories make the 6 o'clock news. However, a courageous letter from Karri Ann Gonzalez about her guardian, a horse named Annie, speaks of the emotional healing animals can offer us, healing that sometimes comes slowly with persistent love and companionship.

I was thirteen when I got involved with an older man. When the relationship began, I was ecstatic, flattered to go out with a man seven years older than me. When it ended two years later, I had lived through a nightmare. He violated me physically, sexually, and mentally. During the course of those two years, I wove elaborate tales to convince critics that ours was a "normal" relationship. Slowly, I had distanced myself from all of my friends and by my second year with my boyfriend, I lived in forced submission, afraid of life with him and without him. On our second Christmas together, he unknowingly gave me the chance to get my life back. He bought me a skinny, haggard mare named "Annie."

Annie was a godsend. For the first time in two years, I had something that was mine alone to care for and to care about. Annie came from an abusive background, and every day I nurtured and cared for her, marveling at her recovery and taking pride in her slow progress. I spent hours at a time just watching her graze, wishing someone could restore me the way I was restoring her. She became my confidante and the more I confided in her, the stronger our bond grew.

I can still clearly recall the day she saved me. I had been out grooming her when my boyfriend appeared unexpectedly. He came to the barn looking for us and wanted to help me groom Annie. I was frustrated at his brusque way of handling her, and finally asked him to wait for me in the house. Already jealous of my attachment to Annie, my boyfriend exploded in anger. As he became louder, more animated, and threatening, I noticed Annie's uneasiness and became more concerned for her safety than mine. When I tried to go to her, he erupted, grabbing my arms and shaking me hard. He hurled insults at both me and Annie, and I distinctly remember feeling relief that his anger had been unleashed on me and not on my beloved horse. Suddenly, he released me and I fell roughly on the ground. It wasn't until I sat up that I saw why he had let me go so abruptly. Annie had charged him, knocking him into the barn wall. Shocked, we both looked at Annie as she turned to me and lowered her head, sniffing me over as though she were checking for injuries. My boyfriend silently retreated to the house.

I can't begin to describe the emotions I felt that day. Mostly, I marveled at Annie's courage, amazed that she stood up for me. Through the defiant stance she had taken against my boyfriend, Annie had instantly reversed the balance of power between my boyfriend and me. One week after that day, I left my boyfriend.

I wish I could say "and we lived happily ever after," but it wasn't that easy. Because of my feelings of guilt and shame, I couldn't bring myself to tell anyone what I had gone through. I was afraid no one would believe me. My boyfriend had drilled into my head that I was at fault for everything in my life, and I had grown to believe him. My deep sense of dirtiness and shame kept me from seeking counseling. I lost every ounce of self-confidence that I ever had. But Annie gave it back. She challenged me daily and I thrived on those challenges and I became a very accomplished rider. Reflecting on my achievements with Annie, I slowly began to see that I did have self-worth. Day by day, I began to recognize myself as the talented, able-bodied person that I was and am. As I relished this new found competence, my esteem grew. Daily, I became more bold and confident, and soon I was reentering activities I had lost.

I struggled through the worst of the emotional nightmares by myself, leaning on Annie for comfort and support. When I awoke in the middle of the night with bad dreams, I would go out to the barn and seek comfort with Annie. I had never gone through such a painful situation before and I lacked the wisdom that years of life experience often gives people. Sitting in the barn with Annie on those lonely nights, I often wished she could tell me what to do.

Annie was clearly my hero. I regarded her with the same awe that a child holds for magic. Determined to repay her by giving her the life I wanted so badly, I demanded the best for her. From her feed to her bedding, Annie received nothing less than perfection. Never did it cross my mind that my relationship with Annie may have become an obsession. Looking back now, I realize that I was simply unable to cope with all of the overwhelming pain involved in my healing process. Subconsciously, I used Annie's restoration as a mirror for my own recovery: The whole time I was consumed with Annie's renewal, I was actually healing myself. Some people have heroes to rescue them—I have a horse named Annie.

PHOTO: JODI FREDIANI

Sometimes an animal's intercession, making the difference between life and death, can happen in the most unexpected way. The one animal who rescued me from the proverbial jaws of death had lost its own life only moments before. As I sped down the road at fifty miles an hour, I caught a glimpse of an owl, motionless, on the side of the road. I don't frequently stop for road kills, but something told me to make an exception. Perhaps the owl was still alive. Besides, I was glad for an excuse to delay my morning appointment for cancer treatment with the radiation clinic.

I pulled out of my place between a blue Chevy Impala and a red pickup truck with no tailgate. As I drove up to the curb alongside the owl a heavy truck whirled by. In that gust of wind, the owl's feathers fluttered like dried straw and I knew that the bird was dead. The sight of the owl's forlorn body, tumbling along the highway like a discarded bottle, disturbed me deeply. To rectify some of that horror, I decided to take the owl home for burial.

I fussed around in the cab of my pickup and found a clean rag. Then I climbed out to pick up the bird. The cars swooshed past and blew what little hair I had left on my head from radiation treatments. The owl was still soft and warm, its great brown eyes squeezed shut. The feathers, unbroken, were magnificently colored, as though someone had painted each one with painstaking detail and care. The talons were limp, the black nails hanging like scythes. A small trickle of blood seeped from one slanted nostril. It must have died only minutes before.

I placed the owl in the back of my truck, mindful that some Native Americans regard owls as powerful symbols. Although I have since learned that owls represent death and rebirth, at the time I believed that owls signified good fortune.

So, before I shut the tailgate, I said to the bird, "And what great, good fortune do you have in store for me today?" Then I climbed into my truck and pulled back into the traffic.

A few minutes later I rounded the curve to the hospital, and was stunned by the sight of the smoking wreckage of the blue Chevy Impala and the old red pickup with no tailgate. Both vehicles were crumpled into charred heaps against the side of a jackknifed, big-rig truck, which lay on its side belching smoke and flames. Sirens bellowed in the air and an ambulance shrieked past me.

When I arrived at the clinic, I had no awareness of having driven there. Through the haze of shock, I could feel the presence of the owl wrapped in the rag shroud in the back of my truck. Even now, when I remember that day years ago, the hair on my arms and neck rises. That morning, the universe touched me through the wing-tips of an old barn owl. That touch saved my life.

I buried the owl in my flower garden. With a pair of scissors, I snipped off several of its magnificent wing feathers and hung them on my wall where they remain today. I still offer thanks to that owl who I believe, knowingly, gave its life for me. It is a miracle that one, small barn owl captured my attention as I sped down the highway at fifty miles an hour, and gently brought me to the safe side of the road.

There are many stories of a mystery dog that guided a person in danger to safety. Late one night a woman called to tell me about a friend who was escorted home through a dark, dangerous park by an unfamiliar black, male Collie. The dog appeared at the top of a rise just as she was heading into the boundary of the park. The park was not safe in the evening, but she was eager to get home and it offered the shortest route.

The Collie ran up to the woman, assumed a perfect "at heel" position and accompanied her into the park. The woman felt comforted by the presence of the huge dog, as it reminded her of a beloved Collie who had been her childhood friend. Three times in the park that night, the woman was approached by rough-looking young men. Each time, the Collie stepped out in front of her with a menacing stance. And each time, the men backed away. When she reached her apartment in safety, her heart pounding, she turned to thank the quiet dog, but it was nowhere to be seen.

Another woman, Terri Gargis, shared a similar story. She believes that "nothing is impossible with God," and in her story, a dog was the godsend that protected her son and his girlfriend.

Two years ago my son, Aaron, and his girlfriend, Maria, were walking home from a shopping mall. They saw a large, red Doberman charging down the sidewalk, running directly toward them. The Doberman ran right up to them and just sat down, staring at them. At that point, they decided it would be best to ignore the dog and keep on walking, since he didn't seem to be a threat. Then the dog walked past them, ran nervously along a wall that was nearby, and came back. The Doberman again took a position in front of them as they continued down the sidewalk. Within a few minutes, Aaron heard a noise behind him and turned around to see boys from a local gang on the verge of attacking him and Maria. The dog was hidden from the boys by Aaron and Maria, who were walking close together. When Aaron turned around, the startled boys and the dog saw each other and the Doberman chased after the threatening boys, who quickly ran off in fear. The dog then came back and took his position in front of Aaron and Maria and continued to walk with them to Maria's apartment.

Aaron headed for home and the Doberman stayed with him until he reached a nearby convenience store, which was in "safe" territory. Then, the dog just vanished. Aaron returned home to tell me in jubilation all that had just taken place. We are totally convinced that this was more than a noble act by a dog: this was an angel in the intimidating form of a Doberman.

When a cat or dog rescues its owner, we call it love and heroism. When a wild animal reportedly saves someone, we don't know what to call it. These are stories that confirm the bond we share with all creatures. They are stories that reflect the words of sages, shamans, and mystics: *We are all one.*

In their book, *The Strange World of Animals and Pets*, authors Vincent and Margaret Gaddis researched and collected unusual animal stories from around the world, and created a book full of tales of rescue and guidance. These are stories to share and to ponder. One concerns a native East Indian woman whose child fell into a river. Unable to swim, the mother screamed for help. A group of chattering monkeys on the opposite shore responded. One monkey plunged into the current, grasped the child, swam back to shore and deposited the child, safely, at the woman's feet. Many other stories in the Gaddis's collection are equally thought-provoking.

Twelve-year-old Rheal Guindon of Ontario went with his parents on a fishing trip. From the shore, the boy watched the boat overturn and his parents drown. Grief stricken, lonely, and frightened, he set out for Kapuskasing, the nearest town. It was bitterly cold and when night came the temperature fell below zero. Exhausted and chilled to the bone, he lay down on the ground and prayed.

Suddenly he felt something furry against him. In the dark, he couldn't tell what kind of animal it was but it was warm so he put his arm around it and huddled close. Then, he cried himself to sleep. When he awoke the next morning, three beavers were lying against him and across his body. They had kept him from freezing to death.

During the summer of 1962, a bighorn sheep came down from the mountains into the village of Mt. Baldy, California. Sick and almost blind, the ewe was found and nursed back to health by a local doctor. When the animal was well, she returned to the wilderness. Two months later, she brought her ailing newborn lamb to the doctor's home. Unable to heal it herself, she had found her way back to the man she knew could help.

Often animals can sense the advent of natural upheavals, what we call "disasters." There are abundant articles about pets alerting owners to earthquakes, hurricanes, tornados, and floods. With senses many times sharper than ours, I'm not surprised that animals can feel these natural changes in the earth's vibration long before we feel the full brunt of it. What fascinates me, however, is how animals can sometimes sense many other types of disasters before they happen. Stories document incidents in which animals have seemingly sensed future events and alerted their human companions to danger. Sometimes I feel a sense of dread or uneasiness creep over me before a traumatic occurrence. Perhaps animals possess this skill to a more developed degree. Debi Reimann shared a story about her cat Missey that alludes to this special perception animals seem to exhibit.

My cat Missey saw me through the hard times of a bitter divorce in the late 1970s. In the summer of 1979, my ex-husband contacted me about some papers he needed me to sign, and asked me if I'd bring along Missey so he could see him again. Now, Missey didn't mind riding in the car and usually just curled up beside me and went to sleep but this time things were different. Missey jumped out of the car and went under it, exactly in the middle of the car where I couldn't reach him. It was very unusual for Missey to behave like that and simply wasn't in his nature.

All of a sudden, a car came around the corner, crashed through a row of mailboxes, and landed in the lake. My driveway comes out in the main road right by those mailboxes. If Missey hadn't jumped out of the car, we'd have been in the path of the accident. After the car landed in the lake, Missey jumped right back into the car as if nothing had happened. He had saved my life.

The selfless love that animals demonstrate toward humans, even if it means possibly facing their own death, is always inspirational and humbling. However, one of the most moving stories I read was about the love of one animal for another in a life-threatening situation. Sharon Meininger wrote a story about Tessa, her German Shepherd, and Petey, the family parakeet. One afternoon during a fierce storm, Petey escaped from his cage and flew into the pouring rain. Sharon's son Mike immediately undertook a rescue mission assisted by Tessa. The winds and rain were so strong that they could see the bird being tossed about in the air, but still it flew away.

Mike felt helpless to rescue Petey, and ran back to the garage for shelter. But Tessa didn't come back, even though Mike called her repeatedly. Finally, Tessa walked back into the garage. She was holding the trembling little bird in her mouth. I'll never forget the sight of that tiny bird inside the mouth of Tessa, an exceptionally huge German Shepherd. Mike reached out and Tessa gently deposited Petey in his hand. The parakeet was wet, shaking, and minus a tail.

We can't begin to know what happened in those lost moments between Tessa and Petey. We had all known that Tessa would lay down her life in an instant for Mike. Maybe she had felt his worry and concern for the tiny bird and acted on it. I guess we'll never know.

My beloved son Michael died in an auto accident in 1989, ten years after Tessa had died a natural death. I'm sure they are together again.

In keeping with the vivid examples of animals risking their lives and well-being for humans, there are times when it behooves us to take risks on our own behalf. If we are open to it, animals can bring us the threefold gifts of risk, adventure, and discovery. With their guidance, we can come to celebrate changes in place, attitude, and circumstance. We can learn to welcome rather than fear change. We can also come to relish risk instead of studiously avoiding it. I first experienced the opportunity for risk-taking—inspired by an animal—when I was quite young.

One Sunday evening when I was six years old, I was camped by our black-and-white TV, watching that great old Disney movie, *One Day at Teton Marsh*. A young otter strays away from his family for a day and has a series of funny and harrowing adventures, much like what happens to us humans when we grow up and stray away from our families. At the end of the show I looked up at my parents, opened my mouth, and heard these words come out: "When I get out of high school, I'm going to get a job at Teton Marsh." I had no idea where, or even if, Teton Marsh existed. It could have been on the moon. It didn't matter. I simply knew, somehow, that it was to be. Mom said, "That's nice, dear. You do that."

When I was eighteen years old, I learned that Teton Marsh was in Teton National Park. I moved there and for the next six years lived in the vibrant majesty of Jackson Hole, Wyoming. Like that young otter, I lived away from my family, cavorting through adventure after adventure. Without equivocation, I can say that those years were the most precious of my life. Why they achieved such stature I am not certain, since I spent most of my time roaming the countryside, working a slew of odd jobs from drugstore clerk to town belly dancer, and simply goofing off to my heart's content. But when faced with what I thought was my cancer deathbed years later, those times in Jackson Hole would come back to me in brilliant flashes of color and emotion and I would say to myself, "Thank God I lived there. Thank God I lived there then."

A few years after my return from the Tetons, I worked for a local humane society in Sonoma County. One afternoon, I accompanied a humane officer to renew a permit for a local animal establishment. This place housed a wide variety of animals used in television shows and movies, including an otter who lived in a lovely pen with a waterslide and plants. When I passed the otter's enclosure, he reached out to me and I spent a mesmerizing moment stroking his dense, luxurious fur and gazing into those bright eyes as black and shiny as ebony. The owner of the establishment said, "Yep, he's quite a star, y'know. You might even remember him from way back when. But, hell, you're probably too young to remember. He starred in that old Disney show, *One Day at Teton Marsh*."

For years I believed I was the only person on earth who had been guided along life's path by an animal—in my case an otter—but I was greatly mistaken. Animals have led many people to their deepest joys and transformations. The following stories by three special women demonstrate how animals can guide us to the exhilarating discovery of new lives and new missions. These women aren't high adventurers or daring risk-takers in the traditional sense, yet they chose new life paths that demanded courage and a strong commitment to change.

I had heard that animals are good for people, that they can change lives. Somewhere deep down, I suppose I assumed it could happen—to other people. In the fall of 1989, I was certain that life for me held no promise. Nothing, I believed, could change my life.

I had recently begun my third year of teaching elementary school in Texas. Looking back on it now, I'm convinced I was suffering from clinical depression. I had many of the symptoms: difficulty sleeping, changes in eating habits, feelings of hopelessness, thoughts of suicide. If I'd had the means, I'm convinced I'd no longer be alive. I spent the better part of each day wishing I would just go to sleep and not wake up, contemplating ways to take my life.

It was during that time that I began toying with the idea of getting a pet. My friend and fellow teacher, Maureen, had been a cat lover and began her efforts to convince me to get a kitten. Maureen's endeavors combined with my desire for a pet soon had me persuaded that a cat was exactly what I needed. It wasn't long before a trip to the local humane society paid off.

She caught my eye immediately. A perfect little tortoise-shell and white kitten in the top cage on the right. The papers were signed, the adoption fee paid, and I became a mom!

My life changed immediately with my kitten "BD." The first thing I noticed was that I actually looked forward to going home at the end of the day. No more dark, empty house. Now, there was always somebody waiting to greet me. I had someone to love and care for, to shower affection on, to play with, and to sleep with at night.

My depression began to lift. My wonderful little cat didn't care if I gained weight or walked around the house in a grubby sweatsuit. She didn't care if I'd had a bad day at school or looked a mess. She loved me unconditionally—and at that point in my life, that was what I needed most.

Six months later, I decided BD needed a companion, and so Barnaby came home shortly thereafter. And it wasn't long before yet another, Sunny, joined the crew. Life was indeed good. I marveled at how much these creatures had changed my life. They took a ragged, dispirited person who wanted only for life to be over, and turned her into a happy, lighthearted soul who wanted to live forever. But they weren't through with me yet.

When my father decided to get a puppy, I got him an issue of *Dog Fancy*, figuring it would help him in his new parenthood as much as *Cat Fancy* had helped me. I read the magazine before I gave it to him. An article in it discussed humane educators, those individuals who work for animal care and control agencies and educate the public about responsible pet ownership. As I read the article, I felt what preachers must feel when they "get the calling." My heart raced, my adrenaline pumped, and I knew beyond the shadow of a doubt that this was what I was put on earth to do. Immediately, I began looking for information about how to obtain such a position.

To make a long story short, after several months of dedicated searching, I was offered a position at a humane society in Florida as their humane educator. I spent only nine months there, but learned enough to realize that this is truly my life's calling.

I'm back in Texas again, but my curriculum includes humane education on a weekly basis. My students know the difference between pets and wildlife. They know that animals need love and attention in addition to food, water, ID tags, and shelter. They understand that people and animals are more alike than different. And they are learning to care about the feelings of animals and the feelings of their classmates.

So, you see, animals really *can* change your life. I am living proof! That's why I had to put this story down on paper. Somewhere, somebody will read this and know how three very special animals gave me the will to live and a purpose in my life. All I wanted was one pet. What I got is indescribable, immeasurable, and can never be repaid.

—Patti DeVore

It began in an unexpected way twenty years ago. I never had any experience with pets when a tiny white kitten came into my life. "Oh no," I said. "I'm too busy. I don't have time for a kitten." Twenty minutes later, my life had changed forever. Ruby and I formed an instant bond.

PHOTO: SUMNER W. FOWLER

In the weeks and months that followed, she flourished under my watchful eye and we enjoyed a special communication that only people sensitive to animal concerns can experience. It was then that I realized that Ruby actually represented many other kittens who would never be lucky enough to find a home. I shuddered at the thought—thousands, no millions of animals just as deserving as Ruby. The ugly truth of pet overpopulation slapped me in the face. I knew then without a doubt that I would help animals in every way possible until I drew my last breath.

It was my good fortune to come upon someone selling raffle tickets for a "good cause." The cause turned out to be a progressive new organization which would be meeting soon to plan benefit activities. I knew nothing would stop me from being there. . . .

Steadily, our humane programs evolved and in their formation, I drew upon my experiences with Ruby. The more joy Ruby gave me, the more motivated I felt to give that joy back to the world of helpless animals. The humane ethic invaded all of my attitudes and affected my every action. The purpose of my life became clear, and all my spare time disappeared into that purpose. Years have passed and a great deal has been accomplished, but one thing has never changed. Ruby has remained my motivation.

—*Ellen Sawyer*

It was late summer when I got a frantic call from a friend. She had found two orphan newborn kittens outside of her home. Animals have always been an important part of my life and people who know me just naturally seem to ask my opinion on pet problems. I went over to see the kittens and to help, determined not to get emotionally involved. Well, those two little puffs of fur hooked their tiny claws into my heart and just pulled. The next couple of weeks were a bit of a whirlwind. We lost one of the babies after only a couple of days. We never even had a chance to name him. It was a blow, but my friend and I continued to work with the other little one, whom we named Majik because of the spell she had cast upon us. None of the vets in our area thought she had a chance, but we fought on anyhow and didn't give up hope.

It is impossible to put into words the strength of Majik's little spirit, the way you could feel her life force, and the effect she had on us. The first time she sat up and lifted a tiny paw to wash her face, her first feeble attempts to play—these were truly "Majik Moments." When she began to fail, it was sudden and she left us quickly. She never grew larger than the palm of my hand, but she had become the universe to my friend and me.

This was the turning point in my life. I realized that even the best vets may not have been able to save her, but the "what ifs" still plagued me. Since that time, the idea of being involved in veterinary medicine has never left me. I didn't think that at thirty-three I could just pick up and do a complete career turnaround like that. But slowly, certainly, over the next two years the pull, the calling, increased in strength.

I am at a pivotal point, a major fork in the road, and the signposts are pretty clear now. I know where I am going and I'm determined to reach my goal. I will be a veterinarian. The length of the road only serves to harden and strengthen me, to make me into the instrument I need to be. As I look into myself, I can see and feel the power of the heart, mind, and spirit I will need to attain my goal. But I know I can succeed. I have to. I have been touched by Majik and at the end of the road, the animals are waiting to welcome me home.

—*Carol Mauriello*

Sometimes animals bring us into contact with future spouses, employers, lifestyles. My husband's willingness to embrace the importance of animals in my life signaled to me the rightness of our union. Without Lee's acceptance and love for my pets, I don't think I could have married him. One woman, Joanne Leone, told how her husband found his way to her through her dogs.

I climbed up out of a hellish childhood with the help of my wonderful dogs. There is no question in my mind that I couldn't have done it without them. They loved me so completely—I never had or felt that kind of love before in my life, and so I could not give to others what I did not know.

One day I was out walking with my dogs down on the beach and I met a guy with a Husky on a long rope. We talked as people do with a common interest and he was amazed at my dogs (I had three by then). Not only didn't they need leashes, but he was surprised at how content they were just to stay beside me. We said goodbye and I forgot about him until I saw him at the beach again the next day.

To make a long story shorter, I married him. We've been

together eighteen years. I asked him once why he liked me enough to come back to the beach that next day, and I'll never forget his answer. He said, "I never saw anybody love anything as much as you did your dogs, and I thought how lucky I would be to have someone love me like that."

Opportunities and insights come our way every day in a thousand different forms. We read of places and ideas that spark our interest and invite us into adventure. Daily events can open new career or relationship doors to us if we keep our eyes open. We can take guidance from any one of a thousand sources, from the subtleties of nature to the black-and-white of a newspaper. For those of us who have a kinship with animals, a rich source of priceless guidance beckons with muzzle, beak, hoof, and horn. To follow an animal wherever it leads takes daring and trust. Whether animals lift us out of the depths of despair or jettison us into a brand new life, we have much to learn and to gain by following their lead.

▲ ▲ ▲

Running Free

I took him in as an act of charity. I'd just ended a relationship and was feeling the need to nurture something, and he certainly needed to be nurtured. "Take this dog," said the dog groomer. "His owners don't want him, and he's miserable."

Knowing how much an Afghan Hound would demand in time and money, I took him anyway. He crawled, trembling, into the backseat of my car. When I got home and opened the car door, he bounded away.

As he ran into the wind, silver-gray coat floating, I thought if nothing else this dog named Zack is a truly beautiful creature. Half an hour later, he was at the backdoor cringing, waiting to be punished for running free. When he realized he would be praised instead, he ate a huge dinner, inspected his new bed, flopped down, and slept.

I would soon discover that this time, at least, my impulsiveness would pay off: Zack was going to give me as much as I had given him. He would give me back a cherished but long-lost freedom.

The first time he accompanied me on my regular morning run in the park, the sight of him reduced two young girls to hysterics. Another day, he helped the UPS man break the four-minute mile. Shortly after that, the meter reader called me up and gasped, "That dog of yours has got teeth like a wolf. Do you know that?"

I did not. But I suddenly realized that if his looks scared

that many people, if he really did look that fierce, I could run at night—something I hadn't done in years.

I am a small, middle-age woman, living in a neighborhood that is long on trees, shrubs, and dark shadows. But running with Zack, I no longer have to be afraid … I know what it would feel like to be 6'2" with a voice like John Wayne and the bravado to match.

Now on warm spring nights, Zack and I cruise through the dark streets to the beat of old rock and roll, simpler music from a simpler time. Other runners, always men, avoid us. The shadows float past harmlessly. On the darkest streets, we run in the middle of the pavement and watch the stars. There are a lot of stars in Iowa City, something I'd never noticed before. We are masters of all we survey: the lights, the dark streets, the stars. No one can threaten our domain.

I remember that I once stayed indoors at night. I think of the Central Park jogger. My radio plays "Lil' Red Riding Hood." I turn it up to get the beat and my dog and I run on through the dark. Free.

—*Victoria Brehm*
RUNNER'S WORLD
(MARCH 1994)

Echo Flying

I've never been sure of angels in my life, or of any spirituality, really. But the experiences in my life, when taken as a whole, do seem to be showing me something. I remember, especially, Echo.

I obtained this lithe, thoughtful Greyhound in 1990 from a Greyhound adoption program in my area. She was nine years old at the time, already completely gray-faced with the brindled body of a dancer. It took many frustrating weeks for her to adjust to a new home off of the race track, and she seemed depressed and unhappy at first, so much so that I thought of returning her. Then one miraculous day, I was walking in with an armload of groceries when Echo met me in the kitchen. She was grinning ear to ear as only a dog can do, bowing and popping into the air in delight at my return. I set my bags down, wrapped my arms around her, and cried with joy and love. She had finally come home.

Echo became the most important thing in my life. I had divorced in 1986 and recently ended another important relationship. I was clinically depressed and very lonely. She became the confidant I could trust and we walked and talked several times a week. I had been so isolated with the intense effects of depression, but Echo and our newfound love of walking got me out.

I began to attend Volkswalk events where I met many people. Some became good friends. Feeling considerably better, I decided that I wanted to do more for the special Greyhound rescue group that brought Echo into my life. And I met more friends among the network of Greyhound owners. Echo was the perfect ambassador, showing that an older dog can still have bounce in her step. I enjoyed Echo and the human contact so much that I gradually volunteered more and more of my time. I became a very busy person and hardly noticed exactly when the last of the depression left me.

By 1992, I had become the most active member in Greyhounds For Pets, Inc., and when the president wanted a break from the responsibilities for awhile, I took over.

Prior to this, I never looked outward. My inner pain was all I had time for. I was grieving the loss of men in my life and the difficulty of raising my son alone. Now, we were no longer alone. We had Echo, and we had friends. I had a purpose and goals for the first time in years.

Echo turned my life permanently around. She gave me the true unconditional love we are all looking for. I learned so much about quiet presence, dignity, love, and tolerance from this elderly gentlewoman. I owe her my health and well-being.

Echo and I took our first vacation together, just the two of us, in April of '93. The Oregon beaches were empty at that time of year, so Echo was able to run to her heart's delight. Watching her fly swiftly down the sand, then wheel around to play "chicken" with me as she glided past, is a priceless memory I will never forget.

I lost Echo that summer to bone cancer. As I released her ashes on that beach where we had played, I envisioned her sprinting down the beach, tail twirling in the sheer joy of it, breaking free of this complicated and sometimes painful world.

I know this isn't the story of a brave, heroic dog who saved drowning babies or dragged children from burning houses, but she did save a life. Mine.

—*Brenda McClure*

PHOTO: JODI FREDIANI

CHAPTER THREE

The Soul Menders:

ANIMALS AS HEALERS

Hope is the thing with feathers
    That perches in the soul,
And sings the tune without the words,
And never stops at all.

                      —EMILY DICKINSON

During the first months following my cancer diagnosis, I wouldn't acknowledge any kind of healing but physical healing. I wasn't interested in techniques that could help me cope better or extend my life expectancy by a few months; mere remission or "quality of life" didn't capture my attention either. Full recovery was the only option I would accept and I was willing to do anything, go anywhere, to achieve it.

When my surgeries and radiation treatments were over, I found myself in that frightening twilight zone of life after treatment. The doctors had done all they could and I was on my own to wonder if I'd be alive or dead by the following year. For the sake of my sanity, I tried hard to convince myself and anyone else who would listen that I was doing just fine and that cancer was no death sentence. My motto became, "I don't write off cancer patients." I was ferocious and flailing.

Only two weeks earlier, my lover and I had parted ways. I was feeling confused and frightened about the future. Alone in bed at night, I would look at the white walls and wonder who would want a thirty-nine-year-old cancer patient. Life in my apartment was dismally quiet. Then, Flora entered my life—a skinny feral kitten about four weeks old, full of ringworm, fleas, and earmites. Shivering and alone under the wheel-well of my parked car, Flora looked desperately sick. I grabbed hold of her scraggly tail and tugged. Within seconds my hand was scratched to shreds, but I hung on and brought her hissing and complaining to my apartment. At that point, I realized that my lonely life welcomed the commotion of a tiny, angry kitten who would distract me from my own depressing thoughts.

With the arrival of the kitten, I pulled my energy away from myself and my fretful imaginings and concentrated on healing Flora. Along with ringworms and fleas, she had a terrible viral infection that had ulcerated her tongue, cheeks, and throat. I knew all about ulcers in the mouth, so I sympathized wholeheartedly with this miserable condition. It took weeks, but slowly Flora healed, and along the way we bonded. Soon, she was a loving, trusting ball of black-and-white fuzz who met me at my door each evening when I returned from work. The loneliness of my apartment vanished, and I cherished the success of our health venture *together*. Although my own future looked uncertain, success with Flora seemed to be something I could achieve.

Only weeks after I'd finally nursed Flora back to some resemblance of healthy kittenhood, she was diagnosed with feline leukemia. Cancer. Her veterinarian gave her the same sorry prognosis my oncologist had given me: Flora would most likely die within a year or two. My response was instant and unconscious. As soon as Flora's vet handed down the diagnosis, I wrote her off as a lost cause. Quickly, my emotional attachment to her ceased as I began to protect myself from the pain of her death, which I knew would come. The veterinarian had told me Flora would die and I simply accepted this. I stopped speaking to Flora and playing with her, because when I did I would end up hysterically sobbing for my kitten. It even became difficult for me to look at her. But Flora simply wouldn't let me pull away. When I'd walk past her, she'd chase after me. Her paw touched my cheek hesitantly each night as she curled up next to me in bed, her purr resonant and strong. If my mood was chilly, she seemed not to notice. Flora did what cats do best, she waited and watched.

Her patience finally won out. One night I had an "*AHA!*" experience about my attitude toward Flora. How could I believe my own cancer wasn't a death sentence when I couldn't see the same hope for her? How could I dismiss any being without dismissing myself? Although I was busy blathering about hope and healing, I knew that I honestly saw myself in the grave.

That realization was a profound turning point for me. It was slow in coming, but when it did, it hit me like a downpour of hail stones. How often in my life had I turned away from pain and loss, and from honest feelings? Living at "half-life," I'd put away emotion at the first inkling of loss, and had nearly lost myself in the process.

One night shortly after my awakening, I lit a candle for

Flora and myself. We sat together looking at the flame, and I vowed to Flora that I would love her with wild abandon for as long as she was with me, because loving her felt so good. Pulling away from her hurt, and I didn't need any more painful isolation in my life. In loving Flora, I knew I would find a way to love myself as well—poor diagnosis and all. For the both of us, each day of life would be a day we could celebrate together.

I began a quest to heal Flora that included many of the same gems of complementary medicine I was attempting on myself. Flora got acupressure, vitamins, homeopathy, music and color therapy, detoxifying baths, and unlimited quantities of hugs, love, and affection. Her water bowl had tiny, colorful crystals in it. Her collar was a healing green.

What was most important in this process, though, was the attitude change I experienced from this "mumbo-jumbo," as some of my bewildered friends called it. Healing stopped being so painfully heavy. It became fun, even silly. When I told my friends I might have my house visited by dowsers to seek out and correct "bad energy vibrations," I damn well had to have a highly developed sense of humor!

Over the next few months, I slowly learned that healing is more than heroics over illness. Healing isn't simply an end result, it's a process. Flora helped me reclaim the joy that had died after my cancer treatment and my previous relationship had ended. She brought me tremendous peace with her quiet, trusting presence. Finally, as I saw Flora healed, loved, and cherished, I knew I could honestly hold the same hopeful vision for myself.

Flora is sleek, happy, and seven years old today. Her last three tests for leukemia have been negative. At the time of my *"AHA!"* with Flora, I felt that she was an angel sent to teach me that turning away from love accomplishes nothing. I believe that Flora was ready to die to bring me her message . . . if that's what it would have taken.

Pet therapy, a program that involves bringing animals to visit in hospitals, convalescent centers, prisons, and other institutions, is gaining in popularity. The presence of an animal, even one who only visits briefly, can have a transforming and often surprising impact on residents and patients. A hospice volunteer whom I know takes her dogs to visit the elderly and the dying. She says, "I don't bring these animals in for what many people think is a pleasant distraction or an uplifting, furry interlude. If there is work to be done, completion to be done, the dogs know exactly what to do, and they stay with that person—and I mean *with that person*—until the work is finished. We are there to create a profound space, a healing moment. That's what those animals bring. As a facilitator, I just get out of the way and let it happen."

The work these animals do often happens subtly. It happens with a look, a touch, a presence. Animals know just to sit and be with someone for as long as necessary. When there are tears and grief, the animals do not turn away, as humans are inclined to do, hiding from pain. Author Steven Levine, who writes eloquently about illness and dying, described one woman's pain and isolation in his book, *Healing Into Life and Death*:

She said there were two kinds of people who came into her room.... One kind of person could hardly sit next to her, and when they did, "they used to shift from cheek to cheek, they couldn't sit still at all. They would puff up my hair or put lipstick on me, or thumb through my magazines. They would go to the window and open it if it was closed and close it if it was opened. But they couldn't stay long with my pain." She said they had no room in their hearts for her pain because they had no room in their hearts for their own. "But ... there were others who could just come in and sit down with me. ...."

My request for stories inspired many tales of certified-therapy dogs as well as ordinary pets who stood extraordinary vigils at the beds—or sometimes in the beds—of the sick and dying. Ellen Kaye is a volunteer who often visits the hospice center with her therapy dog, Ellie.

There were four patients at the hospice house that evening who were in the last stages of dying. One of the patients was an old, delightful fellow with a sparkle in his eye named Fred. We'd watched late-night movies together for many months, Fred and I. He was a wonderful old guy who rarely had any visitors, but now his whole family was around him as he was dying. I had brought Ellie along with me that night. Often, she comes along when I do hands-on volunteer care, and Fred's family lit up when they saw her. "Oh, he loves dogs," they said. "Please, can she visit?" I told them that Ellie was a pet-therapy dog and that Ellie and Fred knew each other very well, and yes, she could visit that night.

PHOTO: SUMNER W. FOWLER

I can't explain it except to say that when someone is about to die, Ellie is very cooperative and will do whatever is needed of her. In this case, I felt that it was the family who needed something. I got Ellie up into the bed with Fred, and Ellie began her work, which is always remarkable. Ellie settled down beside Fred, who seemed to be in a coma. In a little while, Fred's eyes surprisingly opened and he saw Ellie. The family got excited to see him conscious, and was in a flurry of picture taking when I saw Ellie turn her head to Fred, and Fred turn to Ellie. They locked eyes for about twenty seconds, and in those seconds whatever it is that happens between humans and animals that we don't understand took place there on that bed.

Then Ellie let everyone know she was ready to get down off of Fred's bed, which she did. About five minutes later, it was time for the nurse and I to turn Fred over so that he wouldn't become uncomfortable and cramped. We said, "Fred, we're going to move you now." As we started this, Fred suddenly became fully alert and said, "Oh, well, one more time I guess," and he grabbed the bar above his head and rolled himself over. We were stunned. The nurse said, "Fred! You're back!" You could have pushed us all over with a feather. And that was that. His blood pressure, breathing, and heart rate stabilized. Today, he is still with us, watching his late-night movies and visiting with Ellie.

Almost without exception, a beloved animal served to acknowledge or even strengthen the spiritual or religious beliefs of many people. In the following story from Michael P. Gabriel, the concept of divine intercession is lovingly evoked.

During the lives of Mr. and Mrs. G., my much beloved Beagles, it appeared as if they would live forever. It was a terribly frightening day when Mr. G started showing tumor growths. The vet stated that nothing but surgery could remove the tumors. . . .

As a Catholic, I deeply believe in asking a saint to intercede to God on the behalf of someone. It is a central part of our faith. With dogs, as with any pet or even wildlife, St. Francis of Assisi is the intercessor for animals. When the next tumor was at a very ugly and bloody stage, I was frantic. Not another surgery! He'd had three already. I knelt and prayed fervently with all my being that someone up there would intercede on Mr. G's behalf. I called upon St. Francis, our Heavenly Father, the great comforter the Holy Spirit, and all the angels and saints. Then I anointed Mr. G with olive oil, much to his dislike.

No way could this tumor have cleared up by itself. Yet, in a few weeks there wasn't even a sign that he ever had a tumor, save for a dark spot where the skin had not grown totally back. Years later, both Mr. and Mrs. G eventually needed to be euthanized. I purchased a poodle pup and named him Francisco, aka "Cisco" after the Great Intercessor, St. Francis.

M any wrote about animals who had reached out to them during moments of overwhelming sadness, animals who intuitively knew how to comfort and console. The following two stories illustrate the magic of such an occurrence.

For many days and nights, my good friend, Carol, had been caring for her dog, Aspen, who was recovering from a difficult surgery. I offered to give her a rest for awhile and care for Aspen at our farm. Aspen died while he was with me. I found him curled peacefully under an old shrub. I knew that it was time for him to go, and that it was his choice, but I felt terrible that he died in my care. It was a really emotional time for me, and I was outside by the shrub crying hard for a long time. I thought I'd done something wrong, or somehow hadn't seen the signs. Finally I went back into the house where my husband Jeff was holding our new cat, Felix.

I was telling Jeff how bad I felt about Aspen, and he went to hand me Felix for some comfort, but Felix didn't go from Jeff's arms to mine. Instead, he reached out and placed his paw on my heart, and he just left it there. Suddenly, I felt this incredible energy and calmness coming through that little paw. It was amazing. I looked at Jeff, and he looked at me and we both knew exactly what was taking place—Felix was just radiating love. He stayed like that for almost a full minute, and Jeff and I sat there bathed in the light of that incredible, timeless moment.

—*Judee Curcio-Wolfe*

This last year has been one of endless goodbyes and letting go— of people, places, dreams. Yesterday I had to say goodbye to two of my horses. One died. The other needed another home. On top of those hard goodbyes, I was still in the process of digging a proper burial site for my old, dear, pet goat. I'd been digging hard in the dirt for a long time that day, when an old brood mare of mine came over to the pasture gate to see what I was doing.

Now, this isn't an animal who likes to connect with me. She's an old gray Appy mix who always keeps her distance. But this day, she seemed to be calling me to greet her, so I pulled an apple off a nearby tree, and went over. She rarely takes anything from my hand, but this time she took the apple, bit it in half, and put the other half back in my hand. Then she turned back to the pasture and started to walk away. Upon seeing that I wasn't following, she turned back and beckoned to me with her head.

I hadn't taken any time to deal with the losses I had faced that day, except to dig in the dirt. I turned and followed the mare. She led me half way through the pasture, and very deliberately turned me around to see the sunset. Then she took the other half of the apple and left. I don't know if anybody saw what took place in the sky that night, but the sun and the sky went through every color change imaginable. For forty-five minutes I watched, spellbound.

The mare had taken me there as if to say, "We know." All the other horses gathered on the hillside above me. My dogs settled in on either side of me, and for nearly an hour we all watched this color show, this amazing transition of light to dark. Each of us said our goodbyes. It was a wonderful gift that mare gave to me, and she gave it in such an unusual, motherly way. Clearly, my horses and dogs brought healing to me when I really needed it.

—Ellen Kaye

Healing is about so much more than mending bodies. It encompasses the mending of broken hearts, lost dreams, and painfully poisonous ideas and beliefs. In *Healing Into Life and Death*, Stephen Levine describes the profound possibilities of the multidimensional healing process: "Healing is the growth that each person seeks. Healing is what happens when we come to our edge, to the unexplored territory of mind and body, and take a single step beyond into the unknown, the space in which all growth occurs. Healing is discovery. It goes beyond life and death. Healing occurs not in the tiny thoughts of who we think we are and what we know, but in the vast undefinable spaciousness of being—of what we essentially are...."

Healing takes away paralyzing fear and gives back power—

a power we can use to mend and build a new life. Kay Sassi's story about her dog, Sunshine, is an inspiring illustration of the soul's reclamation of power.

> In my early twenties, after a suicide attempt, I was under treatment for depression. For two years I received shock treatment and extensive medication, and I never left the house except to visit the therapist. Those are lost years to me now and I seldom speak of them, but I wanted to tell you about Sunshine. She was a small, white poodle with wild, untrimmed hair and an incredibly loving spirit. She was my only companion during those years, and the only living being that could connect with me.
>
> She'd sit in my lap, quiet, as I rocked her for hours in my room. I held her, hugged her, hummed, and whispered to her, and cried into her fur. At night, when it seemed the whole world slept on without me, I'd bring her into my room and she'd keep watch with me against whatever I imagined was out there. She was the only truly safe being in my world.
>
> I'm in my forties now. Years of good health and deep faith have given me what I couldn't imagine at twenty. Sunshine left us a long time ago. Maybe she didn't "heal" me but she saved me so that with time and strength, I could heal myself.

My personal experiences, as well as experiences shared by many others, have convinced me that animals sometimes take on our illnesses or disorders. When I worked for the Marin Humane Society as an educator and community relations staffer, I received many calls from exasperated family members about their animals' "bizarre" or "neurotic" behavior. Especially in instances where these problems appeared suddenly, I always asked the caller if anything new or traumatic had recently happened. Had there been a divorce? A move? A death? Was anyone sick or in the hospital? The answer was usually yes. In so many of these instances, the pet was reflecting the family's stress. A recent series of events on our farm illustrate this.

I am still working on "life-after-cancer," and most likely always will be. Many books offer insight on the meaning of illnesses that strike in certain places in our bodies. I contracted a disease that hit me in the area of communication and expression. Twice, I nearly lost the use of my voice, throat, and mouth. Pieces of my tongue were cut out, and my neck muscles stripped to the bone. My vocal cords quit for awhile after one surgery. It was hard to breathe, eat, or speak.

This past year, strange throat- and neck-related illnesses started hitting the animals on our farm. Our llama, Mandy, developed a mysterious swallowing problem. Simone, our young donkey, was diagnosed with a congenitally constricted airway. Months later another one of our donkeys, Missy, choked on some hay and could barely breathe or make a sound for days. Her timing was harrowing. She choked up twice the week I was to leave for California to care for my dying father.

When Missy started round-two of her miserably painful gagging sprees, I asked myself what the hell was going on. Looking back at that year on the farm, it finally dawned on me that too many of my animals were having ghastly problems with their throats and necks. Because I don't believe in

coincidence, I was left with the sickening possibility that perhaps they were reflecting portions of my own disease or as I
now think of it—"dis-ease" with some part of my life. What
were they trying to tell me?

The night before I was to confirm my plane reservation to
California, I sat in the barn beside Missy. She is a young
donkey, our beautiful show-winner. I cringed at each ragged
intake of her breath as she leaned up against my side. Her
chocolate-colored brow was knotted in distress and her exquisite long ears hung down like withered banana leaves. In the
dark of the barn I sat close to her and felt the nervous sweat
dampening her chest. I brought along a warm towel to put over

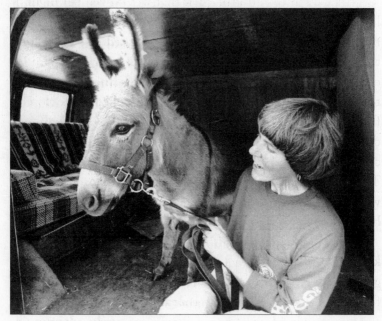

PHOTO: *THE GRESHAM OUTLOOK*

her nose where the vet had run a tube to clear the sticky mass in her throat. Missy was trembling in pain and clenching the muscles of her throat and neck so tight that I was afraid she would rupture something.

Six hundred miles away, my father lay dying. A part of me was almost wishing for any excuse not to go, not to see what I was afraid to see: my father, skinny and sick, weak and dying. Was Missy providing me with a reason not to leave the farm? Or was she holding tight the grief I refused to feel—the grief that stuck like a tight ball in my throat? I sat in the barn a long time that night. In my own way, I was as tense and as choked as Missy, but I couldn't seem to bring the feelings up past my throat.

After a long vigil in the barn that wet November night, I leaned forward and whispered to Missy that I would look much more closely at the hard knot I carried just below my tongue, just above my heart. If she was suffering this pain in order to help me see something that I was missing, I wanted her to know that she could let go of it. Missy looked at me closely for a moment, then nudged me with her nose as she always does to say "hello." She moved forward and pressed her warm cheek to mine and I reached out and held her for a long time. Then, I returned to the house not knowing what to expect, or what to do. Within hours, Missy rapidly improved and hasn't had a choking incident since.

The next day, I went to California and in the ensuing week kept a vigil for my father, who died the day after Thanksgiving. In the shadow of our immense grief, we agreed as a family to spend Christmas together at my farm. I had provided a strong rallying force for our family, so surely, planning a

Christmas holiday would seem simple and painless compared to all we had survived the previous week. But that was not the case.

It is a blessing and a curse of mine to be able to bury my fear or grief in a sudden crisis, and rise dramatically to the demands of the moment. However, when it's time to claim my true feelings, sometimes my "Hero Act" develops a life of its own and I can't shut it down when the crisis is over. The "Hero Act" was in full force as I proceeded to plan our country Christmas.

The day before my family arrived, another of our young donkeys, Simone, went into a fit of choking and anxiety, and nearly died. This episode demanded that I put aside my baking, my robotical decorating of the tree and the house, and my lifeless merrymaking. I also put aside my calm, collected, heroic exterior and called Dave, our vet, in hysterics. When he arrived, I was in the barn hunched over Simone with my arms wrapped around her, sobbing. "It's not just Simone. . . . It's my dad . . . my family is coming . . . he died. . . ." Dave answered kindly, "Yes, I know," and set about caring for Simone. Despite the vet's skilled care, Simone would continue to suffer on and off with a miserable esophageal constriction throughout the holiday season. The day after my family left, Simone recovered. During that week when Simone choked and faltered on what looked like the edge of death, I spent a lot of time alone out in the barn, weeping for my donkey and for my dad. In her suffering, Simone had allowed me an avenue to a grief I couldn't access on my own.

Being part of any healing process can be a profound education if we are open to it. Doug Vernon tells the story of his dog, Jasper, who suffered severe neurological damage when he was struck by a car. Following the life-threatening accident, Jasper required many months of intense, round-the-clock nursing care. Doug and his wife, Jeanne, spent hours each day tending to Jasper's most simple needs. Food needed to be spooned, a small bite at a time, into Jasper's mouth. With no control over his bowels and bladder, Jasper needed to be washed and dried several times each day, and his bedding changed constantly. Bent and twisted almost beyond recognition, the small dog could only drag and roll himself across the floor. Jasper's doctor held hope that Jasper could regain much of his lost mobility, but months passed with little improvement. In desperation the Vernons—who had always put their faith in conventional medicine—decided to see what alternative medicine could offer Jasper. First, they took Jasper to an acupuncturist. The results were so encouraging that when the acupuncturist suggested a chiropractor for Jasper, Doug and Jeanne didn't hesitate. "We were six months from the date of Jasper's accident, and with the help of acupuncture, chiropractic care, and other naturopathic treatments, Jasper was beginning to walk again, if only for a few minutes at a time." The Vernons kept their faith that Jasper would heal and today, Jasper has indeed regained most of his functions and mobility. Looking back, Doug reflects on the changes Jasper's healing journey brought into his life.

Jasper opened my eyes in so many ways. He led me to further explore natural, alternative medicine, and today, although I maintain medical insurance for emergencies, most of my own healing and medical treatment is through chiropractors, acupuncturists, naturopaths, and other practitioners of holistic and psychic healing. Jasper also taught me to seek help for my emotional needs. In the face of an impending divorce, I learned how to ask for help, just as we had done in our search for healing Jasper: Help was out there. All we needed to do was search and ask. A gentleman in my men's group suggested I get some counseling to help me through the divorce transition. It was a great suggestion—I came away from my first counseling session in awe. I was so impressed by the therapist's work that I opted to change careers and become a counselor myself, thus ending a successful twenty-year career in television.

Jasper taught me so much about the power of love. Several of Jasper's doctors have told me that it was the endless love we poured out to Jasper that sustained him through his many months of convalescence and healing. Without that love, they say, Jasper would never have achieved the quality of life he now enjoys.

As Jasper came back from the brink, he guided both Jeanne and me into our own spirituality, our own individualism, and into a deep respect for the unknown. Spirituality plays a larger role in all I do now. With all the lessons we learned during Jasper's convalescence, we realize what a great teacher Jasper has been for us. We can only imagine what we miss in life when we don't pay attention to all the teachers (plants, animals, and people) that are here to teach us even greater lessons.

Lessons from animals often come into our lives when we are most prepared to absorb them. The stories sent to me frequently described incidents of right timing, coincidence, or synchronicity. Rolling Thunder, a Native American shaman, speaks eloquently about the importance of timing: "There is a right time and a place for everything. It's easy to say, but hard to understand. You have to live it to understand it." I believe that animals have that sense of right timing. Susan Erlewine's story is an example of such timing.

Willie, our black-and-white cat, came to us nearly dead, found on the bank of a river that runs through our town. Someone had drowned a litter of kittens, and Willie was the only survivor. That was three years ago and today Willie is a healthy cat, loving, and gentle, and special. Two years ago, though, I had an experience that changed my life, and Willie was the catalyst.

I had been in counseling, struggling with a difficult marriage and with my memories of having been sexually abused as a child. I had always had some conscious memories of the abuse and later had confirmation that my grandfather was known by certain family members as a child molester.

As part of my therapy, I had been keeping a dream journal, waking myself up as soon as I had a dream and writing it down in a notebook I kept by my bed. It was just past midnight and I was fully awake, sitting up in bed with the light on, writing. Willie walked into the bedroom and sat on the floor by my side of the bed. I wasn't paying much attention to him, as I was concentrating on my writing.

All of a sudden, Willie jumped up onto my lap. I was really

startled and suddenly, my eyes welled up with tears. I had never felt them filling, but suddenly, they were spilling over. As the tears began falling onto my cheeks, I could feel my face pulling and changing into a different expression, or really, into a totally different shape. Whatever was happening was totally out of my control. My face felt like rubber. Then I remembered crying out loud, and my voice was different, higher-pitched and panicky. I heard myself saying over and over, "My kitty, my kitty, what happened to my kitty?"

At this point my husband woke up and he, too, noticed how different my face and voice were. He tried to comfort me and asked me which kitty I meant and all I could say was, "I can't see him . . . I can't see him." I felt nauseated, and curled up on my husband weeping and asking for my kitty.

Eventually, I fell asleep but all the next day at work, I felt as though I were shell-shocked. If I allowed myself to think of what happened, I could feel my face start to involuntarily pull back into the expression of anguish, and the pain would start all over again.

When I saw my therapist the next day, she put me under a light hypnosis and gently and carefully asked me what I had seen. As my memory unfolded, I found out what had happened to my kitty.

When I was about four-years old, I had been at my grand-father's house, and had been secretly playing with a neighbor-hood kitten I had snuck into the basement. Suddenly, my grandfather brought a little girl who was about five years old, into the basement. I held onto my kitty and tried to hide and be quiet. As my grandfather began molesting her, the kitten or I must have made a noise. My grandfather turned to look in my direction, and the girl ran away.

My grandfather came over to me, grabbed my kitten and held onto it with his hands around its neck. I don't remember clearly what he said to me, but I know he was warning me to be quiet. Suddenly, the kitten became quiet and limp. He told me to go back upstairs. I never saw the kitten again, but I would look for it around my grandfather's house for many days after that.

Since that memory, I have been able to confirm that my grandfather had a history of animal abuse as well as child abuse. I really feel that the night my cat Willie jumped on me and guided me toward that first flashback, was the night that the door finally opened to my recovery. I have been able to ask my mother—his daughter—about my grandfather and we have begun to heal our relationship. Now, I also have a real understanding of my compulsion to adopt kittens and help them in any way I can.

If it hadn't been for Willie being there at just that moment, I think I would have continued unconsciously to repeat hurtful patterns in my life. I have moved, with Willie's help, onto sometimes-painful awarenesses and necessary growth.

Blessed with a wide assortment of spectacular human and animal mentors, I have always received the counsel I needed if I just waited and watched long and closely enough. Animals have been masters at bringing me examples of courage and joy that cannot be surpassed. Judging from the many responses I received about animals as healing mentors, it's evident that many people agree. This story of a small bird, "Rupa," whose near-heroic determination helped my friend Maureen Keenan-Mason to cope with the effects of a difficult surgery, was especially meaningful, perhaps because I knew Rupa from the time he first came to live with Maureen and her husband.

For being so small, fifty-four grams to be precise, Rupa radiated a large presence. Not many could ignore his uncanny ability to put our three household dogs into a down-stay when he walked from his cage to the window across the room. Rupa was a grey-cheek parakeet with a gutsy attitude toward life that glimmered like a crystal in the sun. In addition to his good looks, he had robust health until the seventh year of his life when he contracted avian tuberculosis. Rupa was given only a twenty percent chance to live, and to live for only a short span of time.

But Rupa didn't die. For four months he lived in our guest-room and fought the TB with everything his weakened forty-eight grams could muster. Rupa survived, but he lost most of his physical strength, forever. He was permanently deformed on his left side often dragging his left leg, and he had to remain on medication indefinitely.

Rupa had numerous setbacks over the years, but his inner strength enabled him to struggle and succeed after each one. Rupa's will to live rang loud and clear—much louder than the ear-piercing jungle calls he used to make but no longer had the strength to scream.

It was Rupa's determination and his inner spirit that kept me going after years of my own pain, which eventually resulted

PHOTO: JODI FREDIANI

in my having abdominal surgery. I was shuffling across the room, pitying myself, bemoaning my weakened state and the complications that had occurred after surgery. As I slowly passed by Rupa's cage, he chirped at me and lumbered over to the corner of his cage to visit me, dragging his left leg behind him. I looked at his slightly askew body as he struggled toward me, using all the strength he could muster just to say "hello." But I heard more than a greeting. I heard, "Never give up. Keep going. Don't look back, deal with it. Life is too short to let illness become your focus." They were indeed the words Rupa lived by. I don't think any card, well-wisher, or medication could have altered my perspective on health and healing more than Rupa did in that moment, as I watched him make his way to see me, taking longer and working harder to do it.

I still have pains from my surgery. When I begin to sadden because I am not "up to par," I see Rupa, dragging his left leg, using what strength he had with gusto, not dwelling on what used to be or might have been. And I do what he would do. I move forward with my life.

I have to rely on my memories of Rupa these days because he died several months ago. His spirit lives on inside of me. And I often wonder if that twinge in my belly is a result of my surgery, or an ache of longing for Rupa to return.

While writing this book, I have realized that there exists an even broader kind of healing, which I had almost overlooked in my focus on personal epiphanies of transformation and restoration: the healing power of nature and our earth mother. The earth is a glorious, powerful ball of healing energy. Left to its own devices, nature heals itself, restores itself, and is completely coded to life. There is a power that resides in the heart of a system, of a species, that is exponentially higher than the power of any individual. The whole of the earth is greater than the sum of its parts. The living systems of the earth reverberate with a generous, restorative balm that we can access in any number of ways: through mindfulness, ritual and meditation, prayer and thanksgiving, and respect. However, the continued survival of this force requires our commitment and responsibility. In his book, *Mourning Sickness*, Keith Smith writes:

In the process of trying to heal my wife Debbie, I became very aware of the damage we are inflicting upon the earth. When you realize your oneness with others, it leads to an understanding of your oneness with nature, the earth, and all of the creatures and processes of the earth. The loss of my wife sensitized me to loss in general. Nowhere is loss more profoundly manifest than in the purity of the air, clarity of the water . . . and health of the animal and plant communities. The cancers in our bodies are testaments to the fouling of these systems. . . . Watching nature and its processes was a large part of my healing.

When we give animals the opportunity, they can reach into our painful, hurt places and mend and soothe. The ways of animals and how they heal us are mysterious, but stories I have heard over the years convince me beyond a doubt that animals are some of the most accomplished and accessible healers we may ever meet.

▲　▲　▲

Facing Up

A dog bit me very severely when I was five years old and I had to have nearly four hundred stitches in my face. He was my neighbor's dog, a cranky old cuss, and he was sick. When I went near to comfort him, like I always did with sick or injured animals, he was on me in a minute, tearing at my face. The next thing I remember, I was on the sofa at my friend's house and her parents were sobbing, "Oh my God, her face … her face …" I didn't know what they were talking about, I must have been in shock, and I said, "What do you mean? What's wrong with my face?" And they thoughtlessly handed me a mirror.

I was in the hospital for about three weeks, and the pain was terrible. Afterwards, people's comments were terrible. I don't think I ever really "faced" that time in my life—I just put it away. Years later in the safety of my talking circle, I finally got the courage to bring it up at one of the meetings. I talked about the accident and the scarring of my face and how this affected my self-image, and my feelings of trust in the world. Our group leader, a man of Native American descent, said, "I think it's time for you to go see Waluna."

Waluna was his white timber wolf. I was scared to death at the prospect, and yet somehow on that particular evening, I knew it was time. So we went out, unlocked the gate, and went inside Waluna's pen. Waluna was a huge wolf with ice-blue eyes, and she was delighted to see me. As we locked eyes, her owner released her from her lead, and stepped out. I was alone with this wolf. And then the miracle happened. Waluna came over to me and jumped up, putting both paws on my shoulders. She never broke eye contact.

The wolf leaned forward and began making these little tiny bites all along the scar line on my face. She went all along its length with these tickling little nibbles, very slowly and very gently. I knew instantly that in her own way she was mending my face. I stood, not moving a muscle, my eyes squeezed shut. Then, something told me to open my eyes, and when I did,

Waluna began licking the scar and licking my face. There really are not adequate words for this: I felt a tremendous healing ripple run through me. It wasn't just my face that Waluna made okay, it was the fear that had been with me for years. In that moment, it just melted away. The wolf's eyes met my eyes again, then she jumped down and left, as simply as that.

After that night, I was finally given the courage to look at all those fears I'd had, and come to peace with them. Over the course of the next few months, I had moments where I mentally relived the entire childhood experience of being attacked and bitten, and it washed over me like some sort of exorcism. The wolf let me know that I could handle those memories, work through them, and that I would be all right.

—*Sonja Homsted Nadeau*

Holy Cow

The calf was dying, starving to death, so we stole her, that's all. I don't know why the mama cow stopped feeding her and I don't know why the rancher wouldn't take care of her. All I know is that I couldn't have lived with myself if I'd done it differently.

There was no question among the three of us, Rachel, Judy, and me, as to what we would do, just the formality of a call to the rancher and a note left at the neighbor's. Then we laid the calf's tiny, frail body on some straw in the back of the trailer and christened her "Susie" after Susan Hayward in the movie, *I Want to Live*. Calf in tow, we headed back across the pass to Pagosa Springs.

We bought all the electrolyte solution we could find in town plus a few quarts of Gatorade. We squirted as much of it into Susie as she could hold and then a little more until her eyes bugged and she let out a bawl. Then we placed her on some straw in the corral and waited for something to happen—a miracle, a thunderbolt, *something*—or even acceptance of the possibility of nothing happening at all.

It was the summer of 1984. Earlier that year, my mother had begun her downward spiral from chronic emphysema and even though she'd rallied after one long hospital stay in the spring, we both knew on some deeper level that death would be coming to call soon. Watching this sick little calf grazing somewhere in the pastureland between life and death, I was reminded again of our duty to love without clinging and to let go with honor. I thought of my mom and a deep sadness settled over me.

The sadness clung tight, so I took off up the mountainside to find a place to pray. Buddy, the Border Collie, followed. "What does he want?" I thought as I climbed and Buddy followed, leaping from ledge to log to rock along with me as I cried out my anguish in the canyon and prayed for help to heal the wound inside of me.

Then, without preamble or warning, I understood that Buddy was my help—a furry little black-and-white acolyte waiting twenty feet away from each altar I chose. He was sent on this day to help me, obeying a voice deeper than the canyon and lighter than the mountain air—a voice my own sadness wouldn't let me hear.

Buddy was pulling angel duty and I understood. Peace settled like a butterfly in my heart. I looked at Buddy and he grinned his best goofy-dog grin, ears pinned back, stump tail wagging. Like old, dear pals, we walked together back down to the ranch.

In the corral where Susie rested, Judy's horses were doing the oddest thing. They had gathered only a few feet away from this sick baby cow to make shade for her. As the sun would move, the horses would move, shoulder to shoulder in a tight, equine sundial, with each horse doing its part—pulling angel duty for the afternoon.

Susie stood twice that day and went down both times, hard. Toward dusk, we thought she might die so we carried her into the barn, laid her on straw, and talked to her about the courage and the space to live or to die. We massaged her and talked to her until long after dark. As we slipped away and back to the house, we decided that if she lived through the night, she would make it. Something else we all knew, though, was that we had to be willing to let her go as much as we wanted her to stay.

Daylight comes early in the Rockies and it did that next morning, sending streams of sunlight through the blinds. I scrambled from bed pulling on clothes like someone late for a bus. In the dusty haze of the barn, sunlight shone on Susie's head, held high with eyes clear as she stood there on wobbly legs. Her black coat, so dull and dirty-looking only yesterday, now glistened with life. I knelt in the straw and put my forehead against hers. "Oh," I whispered, "you are the most amazing little cow." And from somewhere on the softest side of my heart, in that place where memories are held in velvet chambers, I knew I would never forget this time.

Rachel arrived with a bottle and formula to feed Susie and Judy arrived with steaming cups of coffee and chocolate-chip cookies. We sat there in the dirt and straw and laughed at the silly dogs and the snooty horses and we loved the calf and each other, and loved a life that could give us so perfect a moment: the chance to be cattle rustlers and to pull angel duty all at once. And we were grateful.

After my mother died two years later, I noticed how much time I spent watching for perfect moments. And how, in my idealism, I so often expect those moments to arrive on gossamer wings with ethereal-sounding music. Yet it's never that way. Perfect moments seem to arrive in the most ordinary way—looking like cowshit on my pants, smelling like a barn on a Colorado morning, and feeling, once again, as if the hand of God has brushed my cheek and startled me. I do not feel afraid. No, I feel lucky. And blessed. Holy Cow.

—*Jody Seay*

Reflections in a Dolphin's Eye

Author's note: *Kim Rosen pioneered workshops that allowed people to swim with dolphins for mental and spiritual health. This piece first ran in the magazine,* Creation Spirituality.

In 1984 I began leading workshops that enabled people to swim with dolphins and concurrently to explore the impact and inspiration of that interspecies communion within their own lives and communities. In the process, I have seen hundreds of people transformed through the courageous act of embracing the call of the dolphins as an interspecies vision quest—into relationship with self, with others, with the planet that we share.

In truth, my deepest intention is to know the heart of humanity in its mysterious, miraculous process of self-revelation. Every moment that I've spent with the dolphins has been in the name of seeking, knowing, and serving human nature.

Sondra was the first of my clients to explore her love of the dolphins. She was a beautiful young woman full of yearning, imprisoned within a cage of frozen feelings and entangled memories. As she slipped into the water with the dolphins, Sondra's prison dissolved. She became as one of them, dancing and twirling through the waters, reborn into a freedom she had always remembered, yet never known. Emerging from the sea she proclaimed, "My God, they are who we would be without fear!"

Without fear. Is this the call that has emanated so insistently from the heart of the dolphins to the heart of humans since the dawn of time?

Dolphins, simply by being who they are—beings of tremendous intelligence (like us) who live their lives without fear (unlike us)—offer us a reflection of who we might be disencumbered by the confinement of fear. In addition to their vast intelligence and gentle hearts, the cetaceans have another attribute that now fascinates humankind. They have an exquisitely developed sonar system. By bouncing sound waves off their surroundings, they can literally see into and through most objects. This, in addition to their very good eyesight, gives them the ability to perceive their environment in practically a 360-degree radius. The implications are many. Any illness or aberration in a companion can be immediately picked up and attended to. This kind of inner vision gives rise to a society of "no secrets"—for what is the point of putting on a happy face when it is perfectly natural for me to see through it to your broken heart?

Dolphins have the second largest brains on the planet, followed by humans, which have the third. Whales' brains are the largest. Another sapient species on the planet? How long has humankind gazed at the night sky, our hearts reaching out with loneliness for an answer from a distant star, when all the while in our very midst is a society as alien and as wise as any we imagined would come from outer space.

To look into the eye of a dolphin is to look into the eye of an animal with intelligence greater than ours. It is a very different experience from looking into the eye of almost any other animal. This being can meet you!

Patricia came to swim with the dolphins to seek healing from the incest she had experienced as a child. "I will never forget my first swim with Genie, the dolphin. As I entered the water I was shaking and terrified. Genie swam right up to me, looked me in the eyes, and swam underneath me, belly up. She rubbed against me and we began a dance, which she led. She was playful and sensual and gentle. Sometimes she was rough and tumble. She allowed me to gently stroke her side. Sometimes, as she would swim by, I would suddenly find my knee or the heel of my foot in her vaginal opening. It would seem almost as if she were shaking my hand or giving me a hug. Her sexual play was just that friendly, innocent. I, on the other hand, was still terrified, especially when I thought about being so intimate with an eight-foot being from another world. As a sexual victim, I have never been comfortable with touch. However, as we got to know each other, I was able to move beyond my fear and be really present in the experience. To allow myself into an unknown environment and give permission to an unfamiliar being to touch me—without being victimized—was a truly empowering experience.

"Genie taught me that I can choose to say 'yes' to touch without having to be rigidly in control to avoid abuse. This is a remarkable lesson for any sexual abuse survivor to learn. I now have choices: it doesn't have to be avoidance or invasion. This is an issue I've been struggling with all my life."

During the inner journey following her swim with Genie, Patricia found the courage to shout "no" to the abuser of her childhood: "As I screamed NO, my voice filled the room. It seemed to fill the entire universe, and I felt a surge of power and energy throughout my body. It was the first time since the abuse that I'd ever felt totally empowered and totally within my own body."

Genie became a healer for Patricia not just physically but deep within her own consciousness. Such is the nature of dolphins. They call forth those qualities in us that heal and remind us that we are whole: compassion, spontaneity, creativity, truthfulness, and humor.

I no longer run workshops with captive dolphins. Though I miss my dolphin friends, I cannot support their captivity. I believe it is time for people to meet dolphins and other beings who share our planet in their natural homes, where their truest expression of freedom abounds.

My own work has moved from dolphinariums, to the wilderness of the open ocean, to the wilderness of the oceans within human consciousness. For the real journey takes place inside our own hearts and that work can be done anywhere in Creation.

—Kim Rosen

Oh Louisiana Hog Snout Deep

in an ordure of swamp water
surrounded by cypress trees with roots
surfacing like elbows and knees

attended by mosquitos and a mockingbird's
insistent song from a hidden branch
you stand still against the withering heat

beneath shade that is no shade
and streamers of Spanish moss.
Your pink ear does not

twitch for the dragonfly lighting on it
your slitted eyes remain
immobile in their orbits

and you are beyond contentment
or serenity beyond even bliss.
Your rounded shoulders

your bulk and symmetry
incarnate the Great Buddhas of Nara
and Kamakura

and I take this swamp over any lotus pond
this stench over clouds of incense.
All life is suffering.

Suffering has its origins in desire...
T-shirt soaked to my chest
dizzied by the whir of cicadas

I say to hell with the Four Noble Truths
The Eightfold Path
if only for these few moments

Buddha of the Bayou
my heartache falls away before you.

—*John Willson*

PHOTO: CRAIG SOLIN

CHAPTER FOUR

Lessons from the Wild

I would like to learn, or remember, how to live. . . . I don't
think I can learn from a wild animal how to live in particular—shall I suck warm blood, hold my tail high, walk
with my footprints precisely over the prints of my
hand?—but I might learn something of mindlessness,
something of the purity of living in the physical senses
and the dignity of living without bias or motive.

—ANNIE DILLARD
Teaching a Stone to Talk

Teresa Martino is a writer and poet who keeps an ever-
rotating pack of wolves. The animals are misfits she
acquires when their former owners finally realize that wolves
are not, and never will be, pets. While working on this book, I
visited Teresa's home, nestled in the trees of a heavily forested
Northwest island. A cyclone fence circles the forest surrounding Teresa's old airstream trailer, which serves double-
duty as both home and wolf den. To reach the trailer, I had to
pass through the gauntlet of wolves and wolf hybrids and participate in their informal greeting process. The wolves welcomed me with sniffs, bumps, and the staredown. Their eyes
are piercing and their bodies stiff when sizing up strangers. I've
never felt so exposed around a group of animals in my life.

—— 123 ——

Teresa is of Native American/Italian descent and has written a soul-nudging book of poems called, *Learning From Eagle, Living With Coyote*. Several of her poems grace this book. She has much to say about the impact of the wolves on her life, and in particular, her passion for what she calls "the wild." She is alarmed about how rapidly we are losing the wild of nature and losing the wild in our own nature as well. It is a theme she returns to again and again in her writing. I had felt echoes of that loss in my own life, but never had it struck me as deeply as it did that day in her trailer with a wolf nosing my knee and another outside the door demolishing a huge knuckle bone. The jolting contrast between the domesticity of the trailer and its wolf-tattered furnishings and the inquisitive, clearly un-domesticated wolf sniffling along the leg of my jeans juxta-posed wild and tame for me in a manner that still rattles me to my core.

Since that day, I've often reflected on the lot of my life, as well as on that of my species, and what we have sacrificed in our natures for security, safety, the "civilized life." Too many years of domesticity and urbanization have dulled our senses and blinded our intuitive sight. In the process of taming our-selves, we no longer treasure the wild, nor those who exhibit it in their lives. Reflecting on Teresa and her intensity and cre-ativity—the poet, the artist, the wolf caretaker—living in a trailer that is both her home and a wolf den, I recognized the vital importance of respecting the wild in our own lives. How do we maintain a piece of the wild life? All that is fresh, pas-sionate, and creative within us comes from this wild place—

this source that many of us have amputated out of our own lives and fear when we see it in the lives of others.

In domesticating ourselves and the animals around us, something is gained but something powerful and mysterious is lost. Our cats and dogs, tamed to our liking, are mere shadows of their ancestors, the wildcats and wolves. Our livestock animals, docile and enslaved, barely echo the heritage of snorting bulls, thundering mustangs, or agile flocks of cliff-defying sheep and goats. Slowly, over thousands of years, we have created our stock and companion animals in the image we find most agreeable, most manageable. Our creations are easy to fatten, breed, herd, and confine. Now we find the remnants of their once-wild behavior no longer dangerous or fearsome, but amusing. We forgive our dogs and cats their "left-over" instincts: the frenzied, yapping chases after cars and bikes, the intense stalking of catnip mice. Stock animals who fight us and refuse our handling are called stubborn, stupid, or just plain mean.

And what of us, their domesticators? What have we lost of our own wild heritage? When we decry the loss of passion in our lives, is this perhaps the high cost of too much domesticity? When we profane wild creatures, annihilate them for money, attempt to categorize and minimize their intrinsic skills for survival and endurance, we are dishonoring the wild within ourselves as well. Without the wild we are shadow people. "The sacred wilderness is not something just out there," writes author and Dominican priest Matthew Fox. "There is a sacred wilderness inside every one of us and it needs our attention.

We are out of touch with the sacred wilderness of our passions; that is why we see such devastation all around us." Our companion animals have much to offer us, not the least of which is the wise and ancient legacy of their wild ancestors. They also bring us many priceless gifts including cooperation, loving devotion, and adaptability. We need to emulate these honorable qualities of domestication if we are to survive. Our sheer numbers demand a certain amount of taming. But we need to make room for the wild in our lives.

These days, few of us live with wild animals as our neighbors and respected relatives. How many of us have an opportunity to see wild animals living free, outside the confines of a zoo? The sight of a moose browsing in a lily pond or a bear eating berries is a memory that lasts a lifetime. These images are whispers of our own uncharted beginnings. Today, the sight of a wild animal is often referred to as "special" or maybe "thrilling" because we have no adequate words for these rare encounters. One woman wrote about seeing a white wolf in the wild when she was just a child: "I was with my grandfather at the time. He swore me to secrecy because he knew the wolf would be hunted down. That was over thirty years ago. I kept the secret. To this day I feel privileged to have seen such a glorious thing."

In the early 1980s, I lived for a year on a sailboat. My most vivid memories of my times at sea are of the animals—the dolphins, whales, and seals. One night I was blessed by a killer whale. Our fifty-foot sailboat was at anchor in a placid, isolated inlet east of the northern tip of Vancouver Island. We had just begun our nightly card games in the boat's main salon, serenaded by John Denver on tape crooning "Starwood in Aspen." Water lapped gently, imperceptively rocking us from side to side, when suddenly a sharp sound blasted through the side of the hull. It was high-pitched, wailing, and intense. I leaped to my feet and charged up the companionway to the deck, followed closely by my sailing partners. There along the railing pressed a huge, black dorsal fin, glistening in the moonlight like mercury. Our deck was five feet from the waterline, and the fin extended gracefully beyond that, up and over the lifelines. On deck, I heard a sound like fifty skindivers clearing their snorkels at once—the outward blasting breath of a whale spewing a steamy vapor over our cockpit.

At the boat's waterline rested an enormous expanse of black, muscled back and the gleaming white saddle that identified our night visitor: Orca, the ancient symbol of creation. "Oh my God . . ." was all I had a chance to gasp before the fin lurched away and disappeared into the black water. The ripple of the whale's dive sent a rocking shudder through the boat and we grasped hold of the rigging to keep our balance until the water stilled. We all held a moment of stunned silence, and then the excited chatter began. Had the whale been drawn by the sounds of the stereo? Was it singing along with John Denver? Would it come back?

I retreated below in silence. I was amazed by the sheer size of the whale, the utter enormity of its one breath. I had never seen such a dazzling mountain of life so near. The impact was overwhelming. I couldn't seem to catch my breath. So *much* life!

Years later, a friend gave me a deck of special divining cards, called Medicine Cards, that are illustrated with animal images. The description of whale medicine in the accompanying book resonated with my experience: "If you pulled the Whale card, you are being asked ... to allow yourself to be sung to by those who have the original language." I remembered instantly the eerie, sharp sounds that vibrated the hull of our boat. The whale medicine declared: "We are the only creatures that do not have our own unique cry or call. Find yours."

Eight years later, I would be reminded again to find my own voice. Cancer would be the messenger. Had the Orca been the first?

Indigenous people look upon wild animals as living incarnations of special powers, traits, or virtues that humans might learn from if we watched closely and with reverence. Early priestesses and magicians donned animal skins and masks to call in the specific virtues and abilities inherent in particular animals. Rituals and ceremonies in which people acted out or danced the essence of animals have been practiced since human time began. For centuries, animals have served as our bridge to the natural and the supernatural. For me, Oregon writer Roger Fuchs says it best.

> The people who lived on this land before us routinely named themselves for the creatures around them. In these creatures, they saw admirable qualities which they sought to culti-

vate in themselves and in their children. They saw the wild animals as cohabitors of this earth, put here by the Creator not only to sustain life, but to teach us something about it. We are not fully human unless we are in the context and company of our living wild neighbors, learning from them.

How ironic that we name so many manufactured products after living things, some of which are already extinct. The national mascot of our country is an eagle, not an automobile or a computer chip. How much we need to be reminded of the nobility of the animals who live here with us! How much we need to learn. How much we need to learn again!

Unfortunately, some of us believe that wild animals are nothing more than competitors, vermin, or garden pests. But wild animals are simply who they are, for better or worse. It is our fantasies of them as the terrible predators, the fearsome varmints, the "evil" or "bad" animals that live in our minds that tell us about who *we* are.

In my neighborhood, the coyotes sing their magnificent, heartful melodies at night. They are seldom appreciated for bringing the glory of the wild to those of us who nestle along the encroaching fringes of suburbia. No, the coyotes are the sheep eaters. They steal away the cats, the chickens, and the miniature poodles. Some neighbors won't go out at night, convinced that the coyotes will gang up and attack them. But in Native American symbolism, coyote is the magician, the trickster, a powerful sacred messenger who always has a lesson to teach.

A friend shared a wonderful story about a coyote. As she

and her husband were driving home one night, they talked about their daughter, a rebellious, budding teen. They were at their wits' end about how to handle her outbursts, manipulations, and her chaos-causing in the family unit. As they struggled with how to put it all into a sensible perspective, they slowed down for a corner and a coyote walked into the road ahead of them and sat down. Coyotes are common, but those willing to be easily seen are rare. The couple took a deep breath and looked at each other and recognized the gift: Coyote, the messenger. Coyote, the trickster energy. The fool. The one who turns the world upside down. Coyote—their daughter. In that instant, both parents knew they were taking their daughter's wildness much too seriously. Coyote had reminded them to lighten up.

Where I live, the mole is another wild animal despised for its seeming lack of virtues. Many neighbors have a special method for eradicating hapless moles, those rubber-nosed architects of enormous dirt monuments that appear overnight and make a lawn look like a mine field. Yet moles actually aerate the garden and eat harmful insects and grubs. Their hard work is extremely beneficial to the health of the earth. In mystical terms, moles represent the power to dig below the surface. In seeing their dedicated and ceaseless earthwork, we are counseled to work as diligently to uncover what is buried in our own unconscious, to root out our own inner weevils and keep our unconscious well tilled and free of impenetrable clumps.

For myself, I have an agreement with the battalion of moles in my yard. A friend suggested this simple technique:

Speak out loud to the moles in the yard and ask them to stay off the lawns. In addition, I use a small, sonic beeper on a pole as a reminder. The rest of the yard is theirs, I tell them. Mostly, they listen.

Not many of us have opportunities for daily interaction with bald eagles, wolves, buffalo, lions, falcons, whales, or what we generally consider the more regal beings in the wild kingdom. But nearly all of us have seen a deer, a frog, lizard, or sparrow. These animals are no less wild and they, too, have fascinating lessons for us. The following two letters demonstrate encounters that are more subtle in nature, yet carry tremendous impact.

> Twenty-six years ago I was at a family picnic with my parents. My father and I decided to take a walk. I was enjoying looking at the birds and squirrels, when I noticed something move in the grass in front of me. When I bent down, I saw a little frog deep in the grass. As I picked it up, I saw it had only three legs. Seeing this disfigurement frightened me, and I screamed and dropped it. My father picked the frog back up and said, "It is just a frog like all the other frogs but he just works harder to get where he is going." I looked at the frog again in a new light and I saw my father was right. At nine-years old, it may have been just a frog, but as time went on, it turned into understanding, compassion, and respect. It really was more than "just a frog."
>
> —*Jeanne Mann*

My husband had recently informed me that we would be moving to Spokane because of a job transfer. We were not unfamiliar with moving, but this move would be difficult. Our six-year-old son had died suddenly in 1988 and it was the people of our community, church, and school who had gotten us through this tragic event. We would be leaving them and their support as well as a place of our cherished memories.

As much as I wanted to have a positive attitude for the benefit of my husband and my children, I agonized about the upheaval. One morning, as I sat in the stillness of my living room, I prayed for strength and courage, as well as for the assurance that we were indeed doing the best for our family. I gazed out the window and to my astonishment, I saw a beautiful deer! I stood frozen by the window and stared as the graceful animal calmly crossed the street, climbed the steep slope of our front yard, and advanced right up to my window! Instantly, I was overcome with a sense of peace. The gentleness of the deer's expression and the compassion in its eyes flooded me with a sense of calm, washing away all my fears regarding our relocation. At that moment, as I stood before this amazing animal, I knew in my heart that all would be well.

— *Carol Raymond*

A southern Oregon woman sent me an unusual story about crabs she had purchased for supper. I have never considered that the animals we casually select for dinner might instruct us, yet this unusual story demonstrates another dimension of animals as teachers and healers.

During the first screening of Alex Haley's "Roots," a gathering of friends and neighbors at my house ran short of soda, so I took advantage of a commercial break to run to the corner store. Outside, a fisherman stood by a bucket of crabs, hawking his catch. He was eager to go home and said he'd sell the whole bucket to me for only three dollars. I almost broke my arm whipping out my wallet. Returning home bearing what would soon be refreshments, I dumped the crabs into the sink where they scuttled about, clicking and clacking their way up the porcelain sides in a futile attempt to escape.

Back upstairs, I resumed watching "Roots," interrupted only by return trips to the kitchen to refresh drinks and check for escaping crabs. "Roots" unfolded with scene after scene of chair-clinging terror, aborted escape attempts, and doom. Slowly the real-life comparison began to sink in. During a commercial break, I loaded the crabs back into the bucket and headed two blocks to the beach where I walked to the end of a pier to return the crabs to their freedom. As I tilted the bucket, I was suddenly frozen in the glare of headlights. A car full of "raucous males" had parked at the base of the pier. Now I was face-to-face with my own vulnerability: a woman alone, no escape route, and no one aware of my whereabouts. Suddenly, I was the quarry. I thought that if I were accosted, I could offer the crabs for my freedom. But instead I dumped them quickly into the water, mustered all my bravado, and slipped past the men without incident. Upon returning home and relaying the story to my friends, I was met with incredulous looks and laughter. I guess you could say I confronted the appetite factor with awe.

One of my earliest memories about lessons from the wild began the day my brother found three baby robins at the foot of a huge pine tree near our house. He was fourteen and I was eight. He wasn't about to share these incredible live jewels with his bothersome little sister and he rarely let me close to the cardboard box in his basement room where he decided the birds should live.

Of course, whenever he wasn't around to see, I would sneak downstairs to the robin box, slide off the heavy screen lid, and reach inside. I would lift up each bird, one by one, and hold it up to my face where I could breathe in the incredible baby sweetness. Against my cheek, I'd feel the flutter of a fierce heart beat, a rapid-fire of small breaths, pin quills rasping on my skin. Perhaps because I was a child, I knew that the robins were magic. They were from that place of miracles and mystery that I believed would certainly abandon me as an adult, just as I had seen it leave most adults. And so I clung to each moment I shared with those birds, fearing that when they grew up and left us, they would take the magic away with them.

When the robins were a few weeks old, my brother carried the robin box out to our lawn. It was a warm June morning and our mother had insisted that we "get those poor basement birds some sun." The birds were fully feathered by then with magnificent steel-grey wings and orange-spotted bellies. My brother put the box on the lawn and removed the screen lid. There was a sudden, alarming explosion of motion as the robins burst upward into flight. Wings strong and ready, they had settled high in the trees around our yard within minutes.

In those first silent seconds that followed their unintended liberation, my brother and I heard it: The rustle of the leaves whispering the question that hung there in the summer-green trees: "Will you let go?" The robins fluffed out their wings and started to preen.

"Will you . . ." We closed our ears. Two leaps had us at the foot of the trees. A frenzy of climbing, and we were high up in the boughs, reaching out to our runaways with soft whistles. It didn't take much to catch them. They were hungry and didn't know any better than to greet us with noisy chirps and trusting, open mouths.

My brother hurried the birds back to the darkness of his basement room. That night, I heard him tell my mother that he would let the robins go in the morning, and that they just needed this one last night with us. Of course, they didn't need us. It was us who needed them and their wild, mesmerizing bird magic. We told ourselves, "for their own good," we needed to keep them one more day.

My mother arose, as always, at 5:30 the next morning. Outside, the songbirds were in chorus. She went quietly down the stairs to my brother's room, and was the first to witness the terrible sight. There in the box lay the still-warm bodies of three dead robins, their necks broken sometime during the earliest morning hours as they spread their strong young wings and flew up—hard—into the chicken wire.

We buried them in the yard that afternoon. My brother was in tears and as contrite and heartsick as I'd ever seen him. I felt like God was looking right through me, punishing me for my terrible, deadly need to hold tight, to keep fast. We squirmed in our guilt. We two, the murderers.

To this day, I remember those three young birds, their bodies cold and stiff in the cigar box, their once-bright eyes sunken and squeezed shut, and I know exactly what hanging-on looks like.

Lessons from the wild happen sometimes instantaneously and with considerable humor. A good friend of mine attended a weekly women's group that met in the hills of Marin County. City planners have allowed for a lot of open space, and wildlife is a part of many people's backyard experience. This was certainly true for the owner of the home where the group met. On this particular evening, the hostess was struggling with an acutely painful decision, which she shared with her women friends. Her ex-husband wanted to come back. They had not had a good relationship and it had been hard for her to be with this man, but she still had strong feelings for him. She didn't know what to do.

As she shared her story, a skunk suddenly waddled up to her back screen door. Deer and squirrels were common visitors to her yard. Skunks were not. This one snuffled along the doormat, and when the woman began describing her feelings for her ex-husband, the skunk sat up and began scratching at the screen. The woman's story trailed into a surprised silence. All eyes turned to the skunk, who kept up a steady rapping, tapping at the door. After minutes of silence, marred only by the determined clamoring of the skunk, one of the women turned to the hostess and asked the question that was begging to be asked: "So, are you going to let him in?" The hostess looked at her friend and rolled her eyes. "Are you crazy? He'd completely destroy this place. I couldn't even live here anymore if he came in."

The friend candidly replied, "Well then, you have your answer, don't you?" The skunk abruptly turned and waddled back into the darkness. That night, the hostess chose not to rekindle her old flame. She chose, instead, to keep her emotional house intact.

L.E. Reiner sent the following story of a surprise encounter with a beaver who brought an unexpected message of comfort in a moment of grief.

In the early 1980s a Native American friend of mine died unexpectedly in his sleep. I was terribly upset by his death. I drove up to the mountains where he had lived and took a long walk in the woods near his cabin. There was a small pond nearby, and I stopped to rest and cry.

All of a sudden a big beaver popped his head above the still water. He was looking straight at me and it appeared as if he was grinning at me—at least his lips were up and his perfect yellow teeth could be seen. He kept looking at me in the stillness, we two all alone in the forest. I was shocked into immobility and could not move. Time seemed to go into slow motion. And at that moment I realized that the beaver was trying to tell me something. He was telling me that my friend was okay.

In his book *Animal Energies*, Gary Buffalo Horn Man advises, "Animals have been here longer than we have. They are our older brothers and sisters. If you ask your older brother or sister to help you, they will . . . If we ask in a respectful way for help, we humans, the youngest children of Creation, will receive it most of the time." In truth, the meadows, pastures, woods, and the vacant lots of our cities are harboring thousands of teachers. They are more than able to help us. All we need to do is ask.

▲ ▲ ▲

Fox Runs Away

The undulating buzz of the giant cicadas in the nearby grove of American elms was unmistakable. This warm Nebraska evening was August—we didn't need a calendar to tell. The feathers and the broken bits of wing were unmistakable, too. The trail led right up one of the lush, green soybean rows.

Something had attacked and eaten three of our young leghorn pullets. Something had "done them in" and was probably out there, hiding somewhere in that sea of green soybeans. In a prone position on the top of our brooder house, I held my brother's Remington bolt action .22 rifle, loaded and cocked. Safety off. My finger toyed with the trigger. Is it a dog? A raccoon? A coyote? How long can I wait? It had been only forty-five minutes since I began my vigil, and already I was beginning to stiffen up. How long?

Suddenly, in the corner of my right eye, I saw something that was not green. It was red. Red and motionless! I nearly gasped when I saw it. There, right at the end of two bean rows it stood, absolutely still: the most beautiful red fox I had ever seen. I could not believe the fine, sharp features of its face, the delicate shadings of black around its paws, the rich-red color of its coat, the bushiness of its tail. And it was standing not thirty feet from me, staring intently at the open door of the brooder house. Then, abruptly, the tiny predator darted back into the soybeans.

I instantly swung the barrel of the rifle over toward where the fox had been. A second later, he emerged again, two rows closer to me, eyes fixed on the brooder house. Such piercing eyes! Soon, the killer would be mine. I lined up the sights between his eyes and squeezed the trigger.

The tiny click of the firing pin seemed as loud as dynamite, but there was no other sound. The cartridge's primer had failed and no bullet pierced the air. But the little fox heard the sound of the firing pin and his sharp ears knew just where the sound had come from. For the first time he noticed me, and for a brief moment his wild eyes stared directly into mine. Still, he stood there, and I'm sure he gave the faintest hint of a smile. Then, with a flourish of his tail, he turned and disappeared into the soybean field, never to return.

I recocked the Remington and pointed the barrel to the sky. Again I squeezed the trigger. This time, the loud report of the smokeless powder sent a bullet skyward. What are the chances, I wondered, of having a bad primer these days? The ammunition wasn't old. What are the chances? Why?

As I climbed back down the roof, things began falling into place. This was a live fox. A wild fox. This was not some stuffed thing in a museum diorama, or a picture in a book.

This was a living, free, wild creature, running on the land as his kind had always done. And he was beautiful, astonishingly beautiful in the way no tamed or caged animal ever can be. He was alive! Free! He was just the way his creator had made him, and I had been blessed to see him, to look into his eyes. I thanked God for the bad primer.

Walking back to the house, I made another, more stunning, connection. My family name is "Fuchs," German for "fox." I had encountered my namesake. My family bore the name of this wild and wonderful creature, and at last we had met. Face to face for an eternal second. Never again would I attempt to kill one of my kind. I thanked God yet again for the bad primer.

Someday, I want to find a speaker of the Sioux dialect that would have been spoken on the land of my boyhood. I want to hear the sound of the name, "Fox Runs Away," the name I now keep in my heart, as the old ones would have spoken it. The fox I had seen as a teenager ran away, yet not in fear or terror. He paused long enough to let me know he was not afraid. He ran because he was smart. We lost no more pullets that year. The fox had given me something in return for what he had taken away. Now, more than thirty years later, Fox Runs Away continues to thank God for making one primer fail for a moment.

—*Roger Fuchs*

In the Headlights

I was driving south on I-5 through the heart of southern Oregon—incredibly beautiful mountain ranges on either side—when I saw a deer bounding across the median. For the first quarter of a second, I was impressed. But in the next quarter of a second, I realized that this deer and my Honda were headed for the same point on the freeway at the same moment in time. I was thinking, should I speed up, swerve? But I'd heard too many stories of people who, swerving to avoid animals, had ended up as road kill themselves. I was running through my options—there was not a lot of time to evaluate those options. I was going at sixty-five miles-per-hour and the deer was going at a pretty good clip, too.

As I got closer, I could see that this was a very large, beautiful creation of nature, and I was in a very small, kind of aluminum-feeling creation.

It happened. We reached the same point on the freeway in the same moment in time. I'd never been in one of these before but I could guess: there should be a crunching sound (antlers, metal), glass shattering, blood (my blood, deer's blood) everywhere.

We reached that point—*and we passed through that point.* There was no crunching, no antlers, no blood. I looked up in the rear-view mirror and saw these deer feet landing on the freeway behind me.

The deer had jumped over the Honda.

The car was fine, I was a mess. I pulled over. I was just

driving back from having premiered my one-person show called "Life and Depth." The theme of the show is this: Life is filled with moments and the more open to them you are, the richer your life becomes. Not easier, but in some incredibly sweet and magnificent way, richer.

In that moment on the freeway, I knew that whatever I said, did, or thought would be my reply to this incredible moment. I figured I might as well make it conscious, might as well make it intentional. I said out loud, in the front of my car on the shoulder of I-5, "Thank you . . ."

I think the deer illustrates something very important about moments. Not only do they get your attention in some extraordinary way but they also have something to say to you. What the deer seemed to be saying, at least to me, was, "Okay Joe, can we speak metaphorically? You're driving down the freeway of life in the Honda of your body, and you see something about to cross your path. And based on your long experience of problem solving, and problem not-solving, you KNOW this is going to be a mess, it's going to be tragedy, disaster, you know that. Well . . . " the deer seems to be saying, "Maybe that's true, but then again (as it leaps over my car), maybe it's not."

— *Joe Kogel*

Excerpted from *I'm Talking About Being Alive: A Cancer Survivor Reflects on Healing, Self, Money, Food, Art, Love, Death, and God*

Night Visitor

For twenty-some years, we've had a feeding station for neighborhood raccoons. Around the mid-1980s one late evening, a very small, young female showed up by herself at our station. I was horrified to see she was terribly hurt. Her right hind leg was a bloody stump. I couldn't tell if she had been hit by a car, caught in a trap, or what, but she was an awful sight. She was limping on her remaining hind leg and was quite disheveled. The food was already gone. I put more out as she hobbled to hide under a bush. As I came inside, she came to the plate and was immediately ferociously attacked by the other raccoons. She retreated, and this became the pattern.

Each night she would show up later and later to avoid the other raccoons. I began waiting up for her to make sure she got food and water. She came, faithfully, each night, around 1 to 3, after all the others had gone. Her stump began to heal, and she learned to adjust her other hind leg to center her body and balance herself. I hadn't named the others, but I felt a very warm attachment to this horribly injured raccoon. She had become my special charge. I named her Chloé.

My desk is next to the patio doors at the back of the house, and sometimes late at night I'd hear a tap on the glass, and there would be Chloé, looking in at me. She became my buddy.

One evening she didn't show up, and I began to worry about her. Then, very late, I saw her struggling to get to the station. She was using her two front legs to drag her body down the slope to the patio. Something had happened to her only

PHOTO: CRAIG SOLIN

good hind leg. When I saw her, I began sobbing hysterically. The sight of such pain and suffering broke my heart. Here was this sweet little raccoon who already had one missing leg to deal with, and now this. It was so cruel and unfair, I just couldn't bear it. I thought maybe if I could find a way to catch her, perhaps my vet could do something for her.

I stared at her through my tears as she ate her food and sat there on the patio for a long, long while. Then, to my never-ending surprise, she slowly put her two front legs forward and hoisted her back end into the air and started walking on her front legs! She walked for several feet, rested, and did it again. I started bawling all over again, partly because of her plight, and partly because I was so touched by her ingenuity and strength.

This wonderful little creature was trying desperately to overcome her misfortune, and she was doing it.

She got through that first winter just fine. Her injured hind leg healed again. In the spring, I panicked once again when she didn't show up for two weeks—and then she showed up at my patio door with three fuzzy babies in tow! I went nuts: Chloé was a first-time mother.

That was eight years ago. I'm happy to report that Chloé is still here. Several generations of her kits are now my "regulars." Still, I'll never forget that fantastic sight of her doing handstands and walking all over my patio. I never would have believed such a feat was possible if I hadn't seen it with my own eyes. When I am feeling sorry for myself, all I have to do is think of dear little Chloé and I snap out of it immediately. Chloé is a lesson in perseverance I'll cherish forever.

—*Jackie Geyer*

The Puffer Fish

Some time ago after having worked hard for a number of years as a dentist, I decided to take a break and try something different with my life. I had already discovered the sheer joy and exhilaration of being close to nature, especially swimming with wild dolphins in the Pacific Ocean. So I went to live in the Hawaiian Islands for a couple of years. I now had the chance to watch the sunset over the ocean every day and just to sit and stare at the water and see its different moods. But my greatest joy was to swim in the warm waters every day, to join the

PHOTO: JODI FREDIANI

friendly dolphins in their games, or to snorkel around with the colorful fishes of the reef.

This is how I met Kiko, the puffer fish. One day after a wonderful encounter with some dolphins, I was swimming back to shore when, to my surprise, I saw a puffer fish below swimming upwards toward me. This was unusual behavior because puffer fish are fairly shy compared to some of the other fish who often swim up close to people in hope of getting some tasty morsel of food. As I watched, fascinated, I noticed that the puffer fish seemed to be having difficulty swimming, and even had a look on its face that said to me . . . "Please, help me!" Because I have always had a fairly active imagination, I thought I must be imagining all this.

As I continued to look at the fish, though, I became more convinced that it was really asking for help. For many years, I had been fascinated by the idea of telepathy, so I sent the fish a thought of my own, which was, "If you really need help, then you must swim a little closer to me so that I can be sure this is what you want."

I watched and waited. The fish was making a deliberate effort to swim closer to me. As it approached, I saw a large fish hook protruding from its mouth, and a long line attached to it. I reached down, took hold of the line, and dragged up a large weight that was attached to it. No wonder the poor fish was having trouble swimming!

The only thing I could think of was to swim to shore, get some wire cutters, and remove the hook. I looked at my new little friend and sent a thought: "The only way I can help you is if you will let me tow you to the beach. Please don't struggle because you will injure yourself even more."

The puffer fish looked at me trustingly with its large eyes. Slowly, I began to swim to shore, towing the fish behind me. Only once did it thrash about and once again, I sent it a thought to be calm, that I meant it no harm.

When I got to the beach, I secured the line around a rock and raced to the garden for some pliers. My neighbor and friend, Krista, found a bucket to put the fish into, because the ocean waves made it difficult to perform my little "operation" in the water.

Kiko was the name I gave my fish friend. It means "spot" in Hawaiian. He/she cooperated so well that I knew Kiko realized we were trying to help. The hook was too deep in Kiko's stomach to dislodge it, so I cut it off instead. By the time I was finished, Kiko looked exhausted. I placed my hands around the fish and imagined covering it in a big balloon of healing white light, again sending it kind and loving thoughts. Within a minute, Kiko's little fins began to whir around like propeller blades, and it seemed to come back to life.

Gently, I released Kiko back into the ocean where I hoped the fish would recover and live for a long time. I felt profoundly touched by this experience, that I might have saved this creature from a painful and slow death.

Four days later, while swimming in the bay again with another friend, I suggested we try to find Kiko. I mentally called to Kiko to come and say "hi"! Within minutes a couple of puffer fish appeared. I asked mentally, "Are you my friend, Kiko?" One of the fish turned up vertically, as if to show me its mouth. I saw fresh wounds from the hook, and the familiar white spot on its mouth, and I knew for certain it was Kiko. I squealed with delight to see that my little buddy had survived. Kiko seemed to know who I was and kept swimming around me in circles, just inches away.

Our interaction lasted for about a half an hour. It was one of those rare moments, when I truly felt my heart sing with joy. I had believed for some time that it was possible to have non-verbal, or telepathic, communication with animals. In a powerful and joyful way, Kiko showed me that I was correct.

—Inta Rudajs

Tattoo

The little needle hurt as it flicked into my skin. I watched as the blood beaded and the pattern emerged. The color of the marks was a cobalt blue. Blue, the color of healing. The man who was drawing the pattern was frowning deeply, concentrating. He was a mixed blood, Blackfeet man.

He spoke, "Do you have children?" His voice echoed deeply in my ears and I found myself remembering a gathering of people months back. At that time a woman had asked me the same question. She didn't wait for my reply, but told me of her children. I said nothing. The woman asked me again, looking at my old clothes. I shook my head and said, "No, not really."

"Ah then," the woman said, "you wouldn't understand the trials, the pain of separation."

My mind slipped further back, away into the past where

the Grey One stands in the north. Do I have a child? I remember the Grandfather and he smiles in my mind. He answers, "Yes, you have a daughter." Shall I show my daughter to this woman? I study her face.

"I do have a daughter," I say quietly. The woman's face becomes interested.

"Oh? Well, what's her name?"

"She has three names. McKenzie, her given name, The Grey One, which is what I call her in my book of poetry. And her pet name, Baby."

"That's sweet, you call her Baby. How old is she?"

"She is five years old."

"That's a wonderful age, five." The woman was satisfied with my conversation. She walked away, content. Later, she asked one of my close friends about my daughter, McKenzie. My friend then told the woman that my daughter was not a little girl of five, but a gray wolf.

The man stings with the needle and it draws me back to the present. He draws four cobalt blue tracks around my left wrist, my blood springing up to mix with the blue pattern. The old symbol for the traveling feet of a wolf. My daughter calls to me with her heart, high in the northern mountains. I remember hunting with her, the difficult months it took for her to learn to kill successfully. The search for the little pack of wolves she was to join. The pain of separation, the woman had said. The *trails* of life, I now add.

The man finishes the trail of the blue wolf around my wrist. He wipes my blood away, then gently smiles. I take the cotton and later burn it with cedar smoke outside my house. As the smoke rises, I think of what I have been told.

"You have a daughter."

— Teresa 'tsimmu' Martino

PHOTO: JODI FREDIANI

CHAPTER FIVE

Totems, Dreams, and Visions

The one thing that has kept me from being overly depressed and resigned, the one thing that seems to me hopeful in these apocalyptic visions from the unconscious, is a simultaneous and increasing appearance of animals: animals coming, animals watching, animals speaking, animals wanting to lead us, animals undergoing all manner of transformation. To reconnect to the animal, we must become aware of the animals in the psyche ... the animal in things ... in art, in words, in poems, in dreams, the animal that lies between us and the other.

—RUSSELL LOCKHART
Psyche Speaks

For some of us, the animals who reach us most deeply come to us as "totems" in dreams or in visions. Native Americans and other indigenous peoples have been claiming totem animals for centuries, respecting the special guidance, protection, wisdom, and power that this kind of a relationship with an animal can bring. It is believed that totems choose us, we do not choose them. They are the animals that have perhaps fascinated us as children, captured our imagination. They are the animals we enjoy reading about, or seeing at the zoo or in the wild. Sometimes, totem animals come to us in a series of recurring dreams. The inspiration and power we draw from totem animals compel many of us to decorate our homes with images of these animals whom we have accorded a special place in our lives and hearts. We may be chosen by several different totem animals, and they may change over the course of our lifetimes. Totem animals come to feed our souls, not our egos. Hence, not everyone's totem is one of what we call the "noble" animals: the eagle, stallion, bear, or lion. In the natural world, no one animal is more important than another. Even the smallest, most unadorned creature has a unique task, and a powerful teaching to offer us. I know of people who proudly claim mouse, frog, or spider as their totem.

For several years I worked for a wildlife rehabilitation center and it was there that I had my first chance to experience fully the presence and unique energy of many different species. Most species were housed together in different rooms. There was a separate room for fawns, one for raccoon kits and squirrels, another for injured shore birds. Raptors and fledgling songbirds each had their own quarters. Over the months, I grew increasingly aware that each room had its own personality. Each and every animal nurtured at the center seemed to imbue the very walls with its scent, its essence, its way of being in the world. And in those rooms, my way of being was unique as well. I could not imagine treating the hawks like I treated the fawns, or handling the young seagulls in the same manner I worked with the raccoons. Each species evoked a different part of me. In time, the animals grounded me in a reverence for the energy each different animal brings to the world. And I became chillingly aware of an even greater cost of extinction. For every species we lose, a vibration, a light, a special cosmic vitality dies. And when that happens, as it does more than a million times in one full human lifetime, the wholeness of the world is diminished—and so are we.

Gretchen Gould, owner and manager of Herb Hill Farm in New York, wrote to me about her experiences with her totem animal, the crow. Gretchen, a musician and teacher, carved out a new life for herself as an herbalist and medicine woman by being open to an impressive series of events in her life.

On New Year's Day 1990, I took an afternoon walk in the bitter cold. In spite of the weather, I noticed a crow flying overhead who seemed to be calling to me. It flew into a wooded buffer by the highway, then flew back to me again as if it were calling me to follow. It took some doing but I got through the surrounding fence and bushes and followed the cawing of the crow. Suddenly, it landed in the top of a tree. Actually, it was four trees all joined together at the trunk. Instantly, I realized that this tree was a medicine wheel, with each of the trees pointing in one of the four directions. The tree to the east was cut off at the top, showing me that I was short on illumination (the power of the east) and needed to work on that. The crow had shown me my own personal medicine wheel, and I interpreted this symbol to mean that I was meant to follow the medicine path. I have since gradually shifted from a life centered in music to one centered in healing.

And what of the crows? They have never left me. I step out of my house and a crow is always waiting there to say, "Hello." If I take a walk, a flock of them fly overhead. I feel a deep kinship to my totem animal, the crow. And I feel especially blessed to have been chosen for this satisfying work as a modern medicine woman.

For myself, one of the most profound and mysterious totems in my life came as a vision. I call her Gaia. She is an enormous gray wolf with brilliant yellow eyes and a huge, bushy tail that she holds high above her back. From her left ear hangs a single feather, the wing feather of a hawk or owl. She generally appears at my left side, and is clearly the head of the pack that follows her when she visits me.

I found Gaia, or that is, she found me, at a cancer program based on the book, *Getting Well Again*. This classic book was one of the first of its kind to promote daily visualization, in conjunction with traditional medical treatments, as a way to help eradicate cancer. In a nine-week course based upon many of the concepts in this book, twenty of us sought a personal healing vision. I began the program with mental pictures of tiny Pac-Men gobbling up dull-witted cancer cells in my bloodstream. It felt silly and artificial, and besides, I hate electronic games.

Along with the other members of my support group, I was struggling to find a healing vision that would truly empower me. The workshop leaders guided us with the same tool humankind has relied upon for centuries: ritual. Twenty-four cancer patients danced, meditated, painted, and chanted. We cried and wailed together and recorded our dreams. Late one winter afternoon after weeks of this effort, Gaia walked across my mind's eye in all her wild magnificence. She was the image I had been waiting for. Instantly, I felt at "home" with her.

Others in my group found their images of knights or policemen or bombs slowly being replaced by visions of powerful tigers attacking "helpless" tumors, sticky-tongued frogs slurping up cancer cells, stinging black wasps devouring tumors, or huge Orcas swimming along rivers of circulation in search of renegade cells. My Pac-Men visualization changed to images of Gaia and her pack of wolves racing along my veins and arteries, sniffing out and ferociously devouring cancer cells.

To help us feel some of the power inherent in our visualization totems, our counselors encouraged us to evoke and enact our totem after a long day of dance and guided meditation. We cancer patients "became" our totems. The counselors became our cancer cells. The effect of this seemingly simple exercise was staggering. To this day, I remember crouching on the floor, feeling my face change and pull into an extended snout, sensing the luxury of a massive tail plumed high and rigid above my back. My legs stiffened, my haunches dropped. I crouched, uttered a deep, guttural growl, and leaped at the unsuspecting young man who had chosen for that brief moment to become my malignancy. I tore at his clothes with my teeth, lunged at him again and again, and dragged him clear out of the room by the neck of his shirt before he hollered, "Stop, stop! I give up . . . HONEST!" He told me later that my ferociousness terrified him.

I later learned that what I experienced that day is known as "shapeshifting." That is, shifting one's energy to align with energies and abilities of another being so that we can manifest that power in our life. On that day, I felt I had absorbed a small portion of Gaia and her essence.

After my first experience of Gaia, I held to my new visualization practice twice a day, and as time passed the image changed of its own accord. Instead of racing Gaia and the wolf pack through my body each day, I began to meet with them at a special place that took shape in my heart. Each day, I crossed through the fog, stepped upon the old rickety bridge that spans the river, and the wolves and Gaia would be there to greet me. I would sit with them and ask questions, and I would get answers. Embracing my totem animal in my dreams and daily life had become a sweet and healing blessing.

My most vivid healing moment that involved Gaia and her pack took place at a large medical university where I was scheduled to be examined and discussed by the "Tumor Board." These events are nightmares. They go something like this: I would arrive at the medical center early in the morning. First, a slew of interns from the university medical school would practice examining me. Because the exam consisted of sticking a long, ice-cold, stainless-steel implement down my throat, and because these young interns would all be very new at this, I would spend my morning gagging uncontrollably. Then the residents would arrive and proceed to discuss my case over my head as though I weren't there. Usually, I would be referred to as "the patient," or the "white female, thirty-eight years of age, presenting positive nodes in the left clavicle." Finally, the doctors would arrive and alternately compliment and insult the residents. Then, the mysterious "Tumor Board" would convene, and after they reached some kind of a consensus on treatment options, a doctor would come and deliver the verdict to me. All in all, this is not an event designed to make one feel tall in the saddle.

When I arrived on the appointed morning, full of dread and weak in the knees, I was guided to a small, high, exam chair in a windowless room. Then I was left alone while the medical folks organized themselves. Shuddering in my miserable little seat, I prayed to God for some way to get through this awful day. Completely unbidden, a beautiful image emerged. In my mind's eye, I saw the door to the exam room open ever so slowly and I watched as a long, gray muzzle poked through the door. Gaia slowly eased into the room. Her pack followed. The wolves sniffed and dismissed the exam tables and steel instruments and mysterious vials of Western medicine. They nosed the flooring, inspected my chair, and gently licked my hands. Then, with yawns and sighs of boredom, the wolves flopped to the floor around me. Gaia lay by my left side, the side where the tumor had been, and rested her head on my foot. Other wolves curled beside me, some sprawled across the doorway. Sitting a bit taller in my miserable little chair, I felt the reassurance of their company ripple through me like waves of electricity.

With this vision firmly in place, I watched as the door opened and saw the first of the morning's many doctors enter my now-sacred space. I imagined each doctor having to step over my magnificent protectors in the doorway, who watched these "medical authorities" with mild disinterest. Power surged up through my wobbly knees. And in that moment, in that vision, the day became totally mine. The exam chair was suddenly a throne, and I was no longer the patient cowering: I was the queen receiving my visitors. I accepted no medical diminishment, no depersonalizing. I asked questions, challenged experts, made my own emphatic choices, and never felt stronger in my life. When I left the facility late that afternoon, it was with my soul intact and my wolves romping alongside me.

Gaia and her wolf pack are still with me whenever I need their help. Knowing that they come, and that their arrival always boosts my energy and confidence, is a mystery that I am happy to own.

Dream animals appear graphically and repeatedly for many people. Dreaming time is a rich and diverse landscape offering an entirely new world of experience and possibilities. Although a lifelong vivid dreamer, I had managed, because of what I like to call "not enough time," to relegate my nightly dream excursions to a level of minor-to-no importance. I effectively dismissed a full quarter of my life in the process. No longer will I dismiss the importance of dreams in my life. Certain tribes of indigenous people believe that dream time is our true reality, and that our "waking" hours are merely a time for studying and enacting our dreams. Perhaps they are right. The visions, the challenges, the wonders I encounter every night in striking color and detail—and sometimes encounter in exact duplicate during my waking hours—seem more and more an important part of my daily "reality," as I currently understand that term.

Carl Jung proposed that animals symbolize our natural instincts, operating through extra-rational means—our dreams. A master of dream interpretation and analysis, Jung has theorized that certain dream symbols, among them animals, represent core emotions and concepts, archetypes that will hold true for dreamers the world over, regardless of age, sex, or culture. *In Man and His Symbols*, Jung writes that primitive societies believed that each person had a bush soul and a human soul. The bush soul incarnates as a tree or animal—a totem—and when the bush soul is injured, the person is considered injured as well.

Today, dreamworkers and interpreters encourage us to consider the personal context of our dreams. The Dream Network, an organization devoted to demystifying dreams by offering techniques and information to empower dreamers, emphasizes the personal nature of dreams. The Network believes that no one but the dreamer is truly qualified to decipher a dream's message. And that the presence of animals in dreams can bring important messages. "Animals are speaking to us in dreams with an urgency and insistence that we must listen to," writes Tima Priess in the *Dream Network Journal*. "They are offering messages of guidance, transformation and healing. . . . Many contemporary dreamworkers envision a world soul, anima mundi, or world consciousness that may manifest in dreams through the presence of animals. . . . But to hear these voices, we need to listen with a set of ears many of us have forgotten that we possess."

When we listen, our animal dreams can guide us down new and appropriate life paths, or into new realms of self-understanding. Priess shares such a dream in the *Dream Network Journal*:

On March 24, 1989, the *Exxon Valdez* ran aground on Bligh Reef in Alaska's Prince William Sound. One month later, I went to see a slide presentation on the oil spill disaster. A photographer introduced his images of dying wildlife, saying, "This is for the ones who cannot speak." That night, I dreamed I was being chased by an animal. It was a bear, who became a black wolf, who became a wolverine. Each time the animals were about to reach me, they were caught around the neck by ropes made from oil booms and were dragged down beneath the water to the oil-soaked rocks below. When I awoke, I felt the dream was an urgent message. All that day, the eyes of the wolf in the dream seemed to follow me. I felt that I was being asked to do something more with the dream than simply interpret it on a personal level. That afternoon, I heard a newscaster on Alaska Public Radio say that oil was beginning to blacken the beaches of Katmai National Park. Officials were concerned because animals were just waking from hibernation, hungry, and heading to the shores for food, only to find oil-soaked and poisonous carcasses instead. The reporter specifically mentioned the threat to the bear, the wolf, and the wolverine. I felt a sudden shock of understanding and alignment. To have my dream animals linked in that trinity made me realize that I needed to honor the connection those animals were making with me. Inspired, I wrote a poem and put it and the dream on a flyer that I distributed all over the country. In response, I received letters, dreams, and visions from people touched by the oil spill and by the photographs of dead and dying animals that were broadcast all over the news.

What began as a response to a night visitation from Bear, Wolf, and Wolverine eventually developed into my master's thesis in community psychology, "Dreams and Disaster in Prince William Sound." It also initiated a major change in the direction of my life. My experience of the traumatic events of the oil spill expanded into a study of collective and individual trauma. With Wolf nipping at my heels, I wrote a grant proposal for a project working with the trauma victims of my generation—Vietnam veterans and their families. Wolf's guidance in waking and sleeping dreams has continued to assist me in the work of transformation and healing. For the first time in my life, I am doing exactly what I need to be doing.

In the following story from Shirley Anne Briggs, her cat Lucky returns to her in dreams to resolve questions and grief she had harbored after Lucky's disappearance and surmised death.

A few years ago, because of a divorce, I could no longer keep my sixteen-year-old cat, Lucky. Due to several well-timed coincidences, I found a perfect home for him, where he was loved and cherished for the uniquely wonderful animal he was. I had visitation rights to see Lucky, and would drop by to see him

PHOTO: SUMNER W. FOWLER

regularly. He loved his new home, and was loved in return. I lost contact with Lucky when it became necessary for me to move several hundred miles away, but letters from his new owners kept me up to date with how my friend was doing.

Then something very unusual happened. I began having dreams each night. Actually, they were nightmares because the same dream played over and over in my mind like the rerun of a movie. In the dream, Lucky was lost and was trying to find his way back home. I would awaken from the dream with the sounds of his loud cry for help ringing in my ears. I wondered if Lucky was okay and decided to write to see how he was doing. The reply letter stated that Lucky had been gone for over a month and all hope for his return had been lost. His owner mentioned the date Lucky had disappeared and I realized that this is when my dream had started.

After I received her letter, the dreams stopped. I wondered if Lucky had been trying to reach me while my conscious mind was asleep. My mind would not rest and I wanted in some way to be shown what had happened to Lucky. Several nights after this, I had a dream which showed Lucky being picked up as a stray and being put to sleep. I awoke trembling and drenched with sweat. I wondered if this dream could be what had actually happened to Lucky. Several months later, I dreamed of a kitten that jumped in my lap, put its two paws around my neck, and rested its little cheek against my own. In my dream, I sensed this kitten telling me that everything was okay, that this was Lucky, and he didn't want me to hurt any longer. He told me he was fine and that he loved me.

After these dreams, I felt more peaceful. The deep grieving process over Lucky's loss became more manageable. All of these happenings seemed difficult to believe, but why would I have these experiences if there were no truth to them? This is the end of my story, but Lucky's new owner had her own story to relate. She grieved so deeply Lucky's loss that her family went out and got her a new little kitten. At first she didn't want anything to do with this new kitten, but then she noticed how similar its actions were to Lucky's. This kitten had Lucky's almost-human understanding and liked the same foods. She said it was almost like having Lucky back.

Then, sadly, the kitten died. It had not been ill. It simply went to sleep one day and never woke up. I couldn't help but wonder if it might have been possible that Lucky had returned in the form of this new kitten. What if he had returned as this kitten so that he could die with those he loved? Does love create a bond that even death cannot erase? This story is not an easy one to tell. I am risking looking like a fool. But I will take that risk if I can bring comfort to even one other person who has experienced grief at the loss of a beloved animal or person.

Sometimes a pet who has died will return in dreams or visions as a powerful personal totem and offer messages, or bring counsel or warning. Many people wrote about pets who had visited in dreams to comfort or advise them, or to warn of dangers to others in the family. Some saw apparitions of pets who had died and seemingly returned to visit their old homes and playgrounds. A member of one of the groups I contacted to publicize my request for stories questioned me as to how I was going to validate the authenticity of these types of experiences. Many of the stories I received certainly seem almost beyond belief, yet they rang absolutely true for me in the earnest simplicity of their telling. I don't believe that validation is needed for many of the mysteries we are privy to in our lives. The fact that these events touched and enriched the people who experienced them seems to be validation enough. I believe there is much truth in the adage, "leave mystery to mystery." In the following story, Donna Rife shares her experience of being loved and protected through the dreams of her departed dog, Reed.

I still remember the first litter of Whippet puppies born in our home and the love-at-first-sight I felt when the third puppy appeared—a beautiful spotted, or parti-colored, Whippet. I called him Reed.

Reed became my first champion. For fourteen years, what fun we had together. Then we discovered Reed had a cancerous tumor, and the sad day of euthanasia had to be faced. It was the New Year's holiday, and knowing I was spending the last days with my best friend was one of the toughest things I've ever done. Thank goodness I found the strength to hold Reed in my arms as he quietly passed away.

For weeks I fought tears and would wake up dreaming of Reed. He had the sweetest way of waking me if he had to go out or if something was wrong. He would touch me once with his nose and give me a minute to respond before touching me again.

One morning very early, I was dreaming that Reed was trying to wake me with his gentle nudge. In tears, I got up to put on the coffee pot, and thank God I did! Through the window, I saw my eight-month-old Australian Shepherd, Joy, in the middle of our swimming pool, so tired she could barely hold her nose up. I had to help her out of the pool, and I'm sure if I'd been two minutes later, she would have drowned.

Another time, in the middle of the night, I awoke again to feel Reed touching me with his nose. In tears, I called for my cat Bell to comfort me. She always would come when I called, but she didn't come this time. I walked through the house looking for her and found her in the kitchen, unable to stand. It was 2 A.M. and I was instantly on the phone to my vet, who met us at the clinic. The vet determined she had a deadly uterine infection, and rushed her into surgery. It was a miracle that she survived. Once again, I felt that Reed had nudged me to warn me something was wrong, and that he had saved yet another of my pets. I always knew how lucky I was to have a dog as special as Reed. But I didn't know I was to be blessed with a guardian angel.

These particular stories are powerful because of the level of courage and trust displayed by the storyteller. As Shirley Briggs wrote, "I risk looking like a fool. . . ." I have met veterinarians and scientists who call upon the guidance and mystery of totem animals, yet cannot risk speaking of their experiences for fear that such admissions could jeopardize their professional lives.

Fifteen years ago, literature about dreams and totems was not easy to come by. Today, bookstores are bursting with information about how to interpret dreams, find totem animals, develop personal rituals and myths, and communicate with animal companions. In this exciting climate of introspection, the ancient and universal wisdom of our animal totems and dreams may find its way into our hearts and lives, once again.

▲ ▲ ▲

Seal, Soul

I dreamed I was in a secondhand clothing store. A large woman with frizzy black hair watched me sideways through squinting eyes. Before I knew what had happened, she pushed me backward onto a chair and began to unlace my boots. . . .

"What kind of a store is this?" I screamed. I was really raising a ruckus. "Give me back my boots!" The woman with the frizzy hair finally tossed the boots casually into my lap. "The sole is loose," she sneered.

I followed her out and onto a ramp that led to the sea. I saw that an underground parking garage had been converted into a giant aquarium. A sea lion swam near the glass, her dark eyes searching mine. One of her eyes was clouded, as though she were partially blind. All around her, bright yellow tropical fish floated belly up.

The sea lion in that dream touched me deeply. Her appearance at the end, treading water among dead tropical fish, interpreted the rest of the dream for me. I understood that the seal was dying. I thought about the loosened sole on my boot and quickly made the connection that my soul was ailing, but I had known this already.

I could not shake the way I felt when I looked into the sea lion's eyes. I had been troubled by a similar, waking encounter with a sea lion as a child, but I had forgotten the incident until I had that dream.

From a pier one day, my brother and I had seen a sea lion

pacing in the water and barking as though something were wrong. My brother and I laughed and followed as the seal paced through the waves into shore and back out to sea, barking as we watched. "What's the matter with him?" I asked my brother. As if the seal heard me, it stopped and treaded water, giving me the same look as the sea lion in my dream. Then, I saw the fisherman's hook embedded in its muzzle.

The images tumbled in my head, a loose soul, a hooked seal.... The dreaming language taunted me to check and double-check the big life choices: marriage, career, children. I felt confined and hooked.

Much later, someone brought to my attention an ancient story that Clarissa Pinkola Estes retells in *Women Who Run With the Wolves*. In the story, a fisherman catches a seal maiden and brings her home to be his wife. They love each other and have a child but over time, the woman grows lonesome for her life in the sea. She goes to the water's edge and tries on her old seal-skin. Eventually, she returns to the sea for good, but not before returning for her child and taking him with her beneath the waves. She tells him that someday he can rejoin her there.

I have always been mindful of the Native American wisdom that says whatever actions we employ in this genera- tion must be done with the next seven in mind, but I had only thought of my actions as they relate to the physical environ- ment: The seal in my dream was floating in contaminated water, but the stagnation I was experiencing was internal and of the soul. I had convinced myself that this soul sickness was a worthwhile price to pay in order to provide for my children. I had been intent on leaving them a legacy of responsibility, but

PHOTO: JODI FREDIANI

I had forgotten to leave them a legacy of playfulness. Like the mother in the story, I realized that I had to go to my rightful element, my place of completeness, before I could show my children how to get there.

I am awkward when I am duty-bound and distracted, but with a pen in my hand, writing, I soar. My daughters notice and celebrate with me. Already, they are beginning to ask themselves what gives each of them joy so that they can find their own element.

We visited the aquarium on my birthday last year. I took pictures of the seals at play, because I want to remember what that looks like. On the way out, my daughters and husband bought me a silver sea-lion bracelet to wear, just in case I forget.

—Laura Engle

Keeping Promises

I got Brut, a black Great Dane, from a very abusive home. He quickly became the love of my life and my main emotional support as well. When he was six years old, he started losing weight and bowel control, and no vet had any answers. He died while I was away on a cruise, and I never forgave myself that I was not there with him. His loss was just devastating to me. After his death, I would keep seeing him out of the corner of my eye, running up the hill where we used to play together. But when I turned to look, he was never there.

Over the next ten years, I left the area and wandered in and out of various bad, abusive relationships with men. One Christmas season I was in a shoe store when a woman I'd never seen before came up to me and said, "He understands and forgives you, Donna. He still loves you and knows how very sorry you are and wants you to learn to depend on yourself, not on other people or things." I just stared at her and asked what she was talking about and she said, "You had a black Dane?" She said he would always be by my side, maybe in body, maybe just in spirit—a guardian angel, if you will. With that, she walked away. I was utterly stunned. *STUNNED.* But after that, for the first time in ten years, I felt a lessening of my guilt and shame over Brut's passing.

I'm embarrassed to say that even with that amazing message, I still kept turning outside of myself for love and acceptance. I had several more years of bad relationships and drug abuse, when I found myself the owner of another Dane. Her name was Dusty. She got terribly sick at one point, and I promised her that if she lived, I'd give up the drugs—and I did three years ago. Then, Dusty had a problem pregnancy and I almost lost her again, and promised her that if she lived, I'd give up food as a crutch. She did, and I'm working hard at it.

... I've come a long way. I've finally learned to depend on myself, to be happy without a man, drugs, or mounds of food. I would like to have a healthy, happy relationship, but for now I'm doing just fine with a good job, good friends, and my "kids": Dusty, her kids Zak and Sable, and my cat Cleo.

—*Dee Kelson*

Coyote Cures Grandiosity

Coyote comes strutting across
the golden grass of her dreamscape,
and she, the dreamer, compensating for the belief
she has no right to claim him,
cries out his name in unearned familiarity—
"Oh, look—there's Coyote!"—then
still showing off for the dream's costar,
and smug as a straight jacket, she follows
him straight into a trap.

The dirt pit is deep and black, and before
she has time to realize what has happened,
the edges around its opening begin to bloom
with the faces of old men. Their unsuppressed
laughter causes her to bluster,
and her bluster deepens their laughter

until their faces are surreal with the cut
of their laugh lines, and the echoes
of their laughter surround her.

It is then she sees the young man emerge
from the dark to stand beside her,
to cajole her finally, into her own laughter
that sends the old men's arms down
to her like ropes dangling freedom.

Once out of the pit, she turns back
to thank the beautiful young man,
but sees instead Coyote leap out
of the pit and disappear into the brush.

Coyote is the dream,
Coyote is the dreamer,
Coyote is the dreamed,
the dream is Coyote.

—Cindy Stewart-Rinier

We come silent
We speak in whispers to your sleeping ears.
We know no language but our own, And yours,
When you still the mind that cries and moans
With words and thoughts.
We stand blackened and dripping in bedrooms at night
We tap at the windows at midnight.

We carry the speech of rocks and rooted trees
That wear the black skirts of mourning.
We scream quietly as we sink, as we sleep, as we die.
We carry the scent of air tainted with poison fumes.
We leave footprints on your bedsheets.
We ask you to listen, to listen, to listen.
We speak in dreams.

— *Tima Priess*

CHAPTER SIX

Going Gently:

LOVE, LOSS, AND DEATH

Old Blue died and he died so hard
I dug the ground in my back yard
Lowered him down with a silver chain
Every link I did call his name.
Blue, oh Blue
You good dog, you.

When I get to heaven
I know what I'll do.
I'll take my horn
And I'll blow for Blue.
Blue, oh Blue
I'm a'comin there, too.

—OLD BLUE, FOLK SONG

Carl Jung said that after we pass the age of forty, all of our issues are really about our mortality. I am over forty now. Many days, I think he's right. If not for the animals in my life, I would have far too few tools to grapple with that inevitability.

Of all the hundreds of letters and stories sent to me, none were as consistently heartfelt as those written about the death of a beloved animal companion. Each letter detailed almost incomprehensible moments of loss with exquisite precision, as if by describing every instant that led up to that death, the writer could somehow come to understand and accept that heartbreaking parting. It is as though by holding a glistening plum up to the sunlight and describing its color, the way its purple skin reflects light like a thousand rubies, we could hope to understand the mystery that makes a plum burst forth from a blossom. To describe a physical death in some way allows us to hold the awesome hand of death and come as close to this mystery as we can get until our last breath is behind us.

A woman whose dog passed away recently admitted, "I thought the loss of my dog would be much less a loss than the death of my grandfather last year. But you know, I feel just as sad, just as lost." What made the situation even worse for her, she admitted, was that she couldn't share this loss with her friends and family. They had criticized her for her grief over "a damn dog, for godsake."

But the end of any life is a profound moment. It doesn't matter whether it is the death of a dog, a friend, or a songbird. Either all death is important, or no death is important. "Having [an] intensity of feeling for a dammed river or a blasted mountainside, akin to feeling for an injured tree, injured animal, or anguished fellow human being, is a capacity shared by a diversity of people of different cultures and education," writes Michael W. Fox. "It is a feeling that reconciles the false duality between human and animal and between humanity and nature. Australian aboriginal elder Bill Neidjie has narrated how his people sometimes feel sick or get a headache because someone is killing a tree or burning the grass.

He reasons that they feel this way because they are 'part of the trees and the grass.' "

A frog is no less alive than we are. To think so and act so is one of the gravest dangers to life. At some point in time, many cultures elected to believe that there are "degrees" of virtue in life. Creatures who are small, bothersome, or tasty seem to have no merit at all. Yet I clearly remember that as a child, before I was indoctrinated into indifference, every creature I found cold and dead on the sidewalks of New York was a loss to be grieved over, a death to be solemnly noted with prayer and ceremony. I knew no distinctions then. There were no categories of greater or lesser death, more important and less important life. Small children know that, yet they are trained and desensitized over time to believe in a manmade hierarchy of life. The heart that can say, "It's only a damn dog, for godsakes," is a heart that can be trained to say, "It's only a damn nigger, Jew, bratty kid, woman, Indian, bum, witch" ... fill in a word, any word. It becomes nothing more than a matter of degree in that terrible instant when we cease to hold reverence for all living beings. Perhaps the greatest tragedy for humans is that at this point in our evolution, we still cannot accept and respect various members of our own species, let alone those of the animal kingdom.

Through our personal beliefs about the death of our pets and the death of many other animals, we can monitor our own progress on the "reverence-for-life scale." I'm not saying that every death we are exposed to—from our child's goldfish to an oak tree to our laying hen—should reduce us to a river of tears, but there is nothing foolish or sentimental about pausing for a moment, with respect, when we see a life end. Neither should we be ashamed for feeling discomfort, sadness, or even amazement at the finality of death, whether it manifests itself in the death of a sparrow or a human being. What greater mysteries own us if not the incomprehensibility of both life and death?

The affection between people and animals is much deeper than we are often willing to admit. We are taught not to reveal our emotions, especially our raw, deep-seated feelings, in front of other people. Yet those of us with pets seldom think twice about how "good" we look or act in front of them. We simply can't hide ourselves away in their presence. Their senses are honed blade sharp. They smell our fear and our joy, they see our discomfort and despair. And that is why we cherish our animal companions: They love us anyway. The loss of such a love can be devastating, especially if love is absent or burdened with conditions elsewhere in our lives.

A recent and painful experience of mine serves as an excellent example of what animals can bring to our understanding of death. While I was writing this chapter, my father died. His passing held a simple blessing: He died in our family home with all of us close by his side. On the morning of his death, I sat with Dad and watched the winter birds gather and sing in the bare limbs of the small tree outside his window. The richness of their songs and the rustling activity of their small bodies stood in welcome contrast to the somberness of the room. The lively birds reminded me that back at my farm, our first donkey foal, only two-weeks old, would no doubt be cavorting outside in the winter sun at that hour of the morning. The phrase, "I am life that wills to live," suddenly came to mind and I became blessedly aware of the naturalness and appropriateness of death, and of life that delights in being even as my father's life was slipping away.

My mother, the local hospice organization, and I worked together to keep my father at home and comfortable. It was a rewarding and exhausting task, but the end was finally close at hand. One morning after giving Dad his medication, I stretched out my arms and stiff legs and took a short walk in my mother's garden. Sabre, my mom's old cat, rests beneath a rock headstone inscribed by Dad only months earlier. I remembered Mom's description of Sabre's last day. She and Dad had dug a grave and written Sabre's birth and death dates on a garden rock. Sabre's grave reminded me of our innate need for ceremony and ritual to commemorate life's milestones. Thinking back on all the animals buried in the yards of my childhood, I recalled the sense of peace, rightness, and completion that accompanied those solemn burials.

When I returned to the house, my brother and his wife had arrived. All of us sat next to Dad, who now lay semi-comatose in his recliner. His breathing had taken on a water-logged, gurgling sound. We were somber and apprehensive. What would it be like? Would there be thrashing? Terrible noises? Smells? What was being asked of us as participants in this pageant of death? Red, the family cat, provided the answers. Purring and contented, Red slept peacefully on my father's stomach. Since Dad had taken to spending his days in the recliner, Red had rarely left his side or his lap unless Dad, tired of the weight and heat, moved the large cat. When dispossessed, the furthest Red would go was to the small table that held Dad's medicines and juice. For the previous two weeks, Red had been my father's most vigilant companion, asking only to sit, sleep, be with him. And in those final hours, so did we.

Dad's death was the first in our immediate family. Yet the devastation of its impact had been made more bearable for me by a seemingly endless, beloved string of animal companions, all long loved and long gone. Through them, I had learned how to grieve and how to let go. In the solemnity of countless back-yard burials, I discovered the value of ritual and altar making. Holding my dying pets and feeling life float away from them like some luminous fog, I came to know through touch alone the glaring distinction between life and nonlife, that incomprehensible moment when a living being exhales into death. Living beyond the deaths of my animal companions, I learned that time softens the hurt and sweetens the memories. And as my animal companions have returned to live again in my dreams and in my heart, I am reminded over and over that love doesn't know death.

That I could write and deliver my father's memorial service in the early days following his death, when the weight of grief can be staggering, is a testimony to the powerful legacy of loss I learned from my animals. Their deaths had prepared me. I was able to send my dad on his way with peace, joy, and dignity.

The lessons didn't stop with my father's death. Months after his passing, and struggling under the enormous weight of her grief, my mother often called me to ask, "Is this normal? Is it normal to feel this sad? This alone? At times, for hours, I can't stop the tears ..." What is "normal" grieving? How long does grief last? As a hospice volunteer, I found that these were the most common questions families who had suffered a death asked. I learned that oftentimes it is not grief but the fear of grief that is unbearable. In our culture, we have been taught to hide our mourning lest it upset others. Few of us understand, until it calls upon us, what grief looks like—how long it stays. If we customarily hide our grief, then where are we to find examples of what "normal" grieving is?

There is great comfort in knowing that we are not the only creatures who grieve. Animals provide many examples of the rightness and naturalness of mourning. I have frequently seen animals mourn the loss of human family members and animal friends. Sometimes their grief is intense, sometimes it is a quiet sadness that lasts for a prolonged period. In these displays of grief, animals show us the normalcy and necessity of mourning. When we recognize an animal companion's sadness at the loss of a close family member or animal friend, we are reminded that mourning has its own timetable. We must somehow learn to respect the process and understand that it is good.

For years Sabre shared a special relationship with Mom's little dog, Kina. Snuggled together in the evenings, Sabre gently licked Kina's ears as he slept. During the day, Sabre followed Kina around the yard on his daily treks, rubbed up against his chin with purrs, and curled her long tail around his neck. When Kina was old and troubled by painful arthritis, euthanasia seemed the most caring choice for him. In the days following his death, Sabre looked everywhere for her old friend. She couldn't seem to settle down for more than a moment before again searching in all Kina's haunts. As the weeks passed, she didn't return to her old routine. Instead, she would follow my mother, yowling for hours. Mom told me that Sabre seemed lost. Over time, Sabre's face assumed a pensive, distant expression. Much of the time, she slept off in a corner by herself. Sometimes when she heard a dog chain clinking, she would rush out to the yard wide-eyed and hopeful, only to turn her back on the passing stray dog. Sabre never seemed to get over the loss of Kina, her friend.

The following letter from Kathryn Joseph describes a grieving experience that involved her horse. Her story affected me deeply.

PHOTO: JODI FREDIANI

Echo, my old mare, died this year. My concern turned to Pride, my nine-year-old mare, because I knew she'd be lost without her companion and friend. I would like to share with you a very unusual experience that happened the day after Echo's death.

I had stayed with Pride the afternoon we lost Echo. She never ran the fenceline looking for her pasture-mate. She only nickered a deep sound of loss and grief that chilled me to the bone. Like me, she was mourning the loss of her friend. The next morning I put hay out in Pride's field and sat for awhile curled in a ball by the fence. I cried and felt a flood of emotions, from anger to hurt, to loss and denial. Pride stood very close to me with her head down and her nose in the hay, but not eating. Soon, I saw her eyes fill with moisture and her bottom lip begin to quiver. If horses can cry, then that is what Pride was doing. She moved in very close to me and suddenly her legs buckled and she crashed to the ground. At first I thought that something was terribly wrong, but soon I realized that she was feeling everything that I was, and that she, too, needed a friend. For two hours, she laid next to me, leaning her head back in my lap, allowing me to gently stroke her face. During those hours, I experienced a deep, healing closeness with my horse. It was a miracle and a blessing. When Pride finally got up, she nudged me to get up as well.

Over the next few days, I watched Pride quietly mourn for her friend. She stood outside, not wanting to be in her stall, which I'm sure held the same emptiness for her as it did for me. I owe Pride much for all that she has been for me, so after allowing her time to grieve, we brought home Tessie, a Shetland pony. The look on Pride's face lifted my heart and I knew immediately that Pride had found a new friend.

Because animals usually have much shorter life spans than humans, their deaths are often the first we encounter. And it is most often as children that we feel the first sharp sting of death through the loss of a dog, cat, or wild creature found dead in the yard. As children we learn death's finality by watching its stillness; by touching and stroking, again and again, the familiar and beloved companion who no longer responds; by lifting the limp body and knowing "dead weight" for the first time. As children, we intuit the gravity of death. In our respectful burials of our first-seen dead, we acknowledge the power and the mystery of this visitor who will one day return for us. When I was a child, I wanted to touch the dead—the bird, rabbit, or mouse—and somehow feel what death was: the coldness, the skin that felt like hardening clay, the clouded eyes that no longer blinked when touched. Through touch, I fully grasped the finality of death in a physical body. One curious touch was all it took to convince me that there was no way life would return to this empty, stiff container. We learn how to let go when we must eventually take the cold, stiff body and put it in the earth. Without inhibition or judgment, children learn to create a solemn ritual as a way to come to terms with a life passage. Backyard burials of animals offer a lifetime of lessons: selecting the final "resting spot," digging the grave, wrapping the lifeless and sometimes broken body in a makeshift shroud, selecting a few special toys or foods to bury along with the body, fashioning a gravestone or marker, offering candles and prayers for the journey. All of these are sacred ceremonies that spontaneously evolve at our first sight of death. Perhaps we carry within us the ancient ways to welcome death. As civilization moves us away from accepting death as an undeniable part of life, animals offer us unique opportunities to consider how we might face the death of a loved one, or ultimately, our own death.

Those who wrote about the death of a treasured pet spoke of the catharsis and the healing that came from putting their loss into written words. Writing about such an event is also a ritual. When I wrote about Keesha's death on the afternoon that she died, I had the distinct feeling that I was releasing her soul with my pen. Keesha died on February 17, 1981. She was just over ten years old. I always told people that when Keesha died, my life would never be the same. I was right. Life has been good again, wonderful even, but certainly never the same.

That final morning when Keesha faced me on trembling legs and quickly—apologetically—vomited up her breakfast, I knew decision time had come. Tumors had sprouted rapidly along her neck and on the top of her head. Growing like yeast, the bumps were visibly larger by evening than they had been that morning. The pain killers no longer worked. Reluctantly I asked her, "Is it time, Keesha?" She looked at me with her still-bright eyes, turned away, and began a slow plodding walk to my car, as if to say, "It's time." I was an educator at the Marin Humane Society, so we headed there to say our last goodbyes.

PHOTO: JODI FREDIANI

In a stupor, I followed Keesha as she limped slowly through the maze of cars in the parking lot and into my office. Although numb, I was keenly aware that this choice was hers and that she knew exactly what she was doing. The front-desk staff had seen Keesha trudge in and immediately called the kennel manager. Everyone at the shelter knew of Keesha's illness. I drew the drapes in my office and waited.

Our kennel manager, Patti, soon appeared with the bottle of euthanol and a syringe. There was some awkward, self-conscious fumbling with needles and clippers as we prepared ourselves and Keesha for the inevitable. Then, with Patti kneeling close by, I held Keesha tight against me in an embrace I never wanted to end. I kissed the top of her head, breathed in her sweet-smelling dog warmth, and told her how much I loved her. She flinched just slightly as the needle pierced the skin of her leg. She tucked her head under my arm as she always did whenever she got an injection. Patti looked up at me and depressed the plunger, pushing the liquid into Keesha's vein. In that next instant, every molecule of my being screamed out, "No, no—WAIT!!" But there was no waiting. Keesha sighed and sagged in my arms, gone instantly. Patti left in tears.

As the shadows of the day lengthened, I sat there stroking Keesha, crying, and talking to her. Gently, I touched the tumors that stood like small, gnarled mountains on her skin. I held her head on my lap and looked into her mouth at the ragged hole in her palate where the malignancy had started. I stroked her velvet ears and the thick ruff of fur around her neck. With my index finger, I tentatively touched the glassy sheen of her iris, feeling myself flinch when she did not. I pressed my knuckles into the pads of her feet and ran my fingertips along the sharpness of her toenails. All these things I did to commit every blessed particle of her to memory. The pain growing in my chest expanded into a massive, leaden ball and I sagged forward under the weight of it. I gasped for air, and there wasn't enough. There could never be enough.

Returning home late that afternoon, I gave Keesha's last bag of dog food to my landlord and donated her favorite chew bone to the neighborhood dogs. Then I wrote in my journal:

> When I die someday, it will be Keesha who first greets me on the other side, tail waving, voicing joyously, to welcome me home. Then, I will hold her again, and I will never, ever let her go.

Years later, I would lean on Keesha's final lesson about peaceful, gentle leave-taking when my own medical prognosis of cancer indicated that I'd be seeing Keesha sooner than I would have thought. For me, facing that moment in life, my imminent death, was horrifying beyond belief. My whole being seemed to collapse under the hideous weight of my doctor's words, "I'm sorry, the cancer is back. And it will just keep coming back...." At those words, my legs turned to fluid and I felt as though I were flailing under black water, unable to breathe. My worst fear was that I'd become hysterical and inconsolable at the end of my life. At that point, my only consolation was Keesha. In memory, I returned to that last day of ours over and over, not in terms of my pain but of her simple and elegant grace, and acceptance of her path.

Many letters I received described special animals who had been a tremendous comfort when family members were dying or had died. People wrote eloquently of the devotion, tenderness, and intuitiveness of pets who stood in final vigil. The last hours of life can be magical, and there is something healing in the act of waiting, of standing respectful watch or "angel duty," as one writer put it. Joy Manciero wrote about Rusty, a dog who served as a companion to her ailing father.

He came to us full of fleas and full of love. One couldn't ask for a more faithful friend. Rusty was always at Dad's side. As Dad's health worsened, there were many days when he stayed in bed. Rusty would lie by the bed and check on Dad every time he moved. In the days following Dad's death, we often found Rusty sitting next to the bed with his head resting where Dad used to lie. Some days, he would stare at the door, waiting. Dad was buried holding in his hands a picture of his best friend, Rusty. I look at photos taken of Dad over his last couple years, and the only ones I find of Dad smiling are those of him with his beloved dog. I can't thank this angel of a dog enough for making my Dad so happy.

Debbie Sorenson wrote about a different kind of vigil, the solemn ceremony of the funeral procession.

I had heard stories at the hospital about a mysterious, sad-eyed dog who attended several funerals at the local cemetery, and his presence gave comfort to the grieving families. Imagine my

surprise when I witnessed my own Basset, Barney, slip his collar
when a funeral procession turned down the road past my house.
A spot was immediately made for him in the procession—the
mystery dog. Barney followed the hearse to the cemetery, sat
with the family through the service, then returned home.

In periods of overwhelming loss or grief, just feeding and inter-
acting with my animal companions has taken me outside of
my pain for a moment and given me a welcome breather. I
return to my sorrow renewed and refueled by these necessary
moments of caregiving. Teresa Braun echoes these sentiments.

We found a tiny abandoned Foxhound-Beagle puppy outside
our yard. While frantically searching to find him a good home,
tragedy struck our family: My husband's father suddenly died.
This was such a shock and terrible loss for us that our lives for
the next few days were totally turned around. We spent every
day—all day long—with my mother-in-law trying to help her
prepare for the funeral. When we would come home at night,
emotionally and physically drained, we were met at the door by
this lively little puppy. He offered us love and caused us to
focus our attention on him, allowing us to forget for a moment
our terrible pain. Needless to say, we found a home for him and
it was our home. This puppy is now called Pooh Bear, and he
was and is our healing angel.

Of all that I've read about the loss of a beloved animal, one
story in particular stays with me. Jerrie Lawhorne wrote me

about her dog, Pepper, years ago when my article about Keesha was first published. I would pull Jerrie's letter and poem from my files and read them to friends, and we would dissolve into tears and say, "Yes, yes, that's how it is." Even more than a story about a companion's death, Pepper's story speaks deeply to me about the value of ritual in the face of loss. Using a process older than time, Jerrie instinctively gathered precious treasures, objects laden with meaning and memory, and laid these items beside Pepper for his death journey. How long has this unique form of comfort in bereavement—sending loved ones off with food, drink, and treasures—been practiced? Jerrie's personalized ceremony of Pepper's death and burial illustrates the special and tender love that a human and an animal can share as fellow travelers in this world.

Finally this week, after much prayer, I knew the time had come to let him go. So with the help of Pepper's friend and vet . . . I sat in our green rocker and, holding him in my arms, watched as the shot was given that eased him out of a life of pain and discomfort into one of peace and stillness. I hope he felt my lips against his head telling him how much I loved him.

I held him close and rocked him until the warmth left his body. Finally and reluctantly, I placed him in one of my robes, a well-worn blue one that still had my smell on it. I put Pepper's little red sweater on him; the ground is cold. And then I brushed his ears one last time. Between his paws I put two rawhide chews which he had once laid at my feet and gnawed on, and a yellow squeak toy which he used to bring to me, squeaking it loudly.

And finally, I placed beneath him pictures of all of us, the people who had loved him. At his head, I placed a picture of him and me together. I don't need that picture anymore. It will always be engraved on my heart. . . .

I buried Pepper beneath the Rose of Sharon tree in the yard. It's close to the house and I can see it from my kitchen window. Before I placed Pepper in his grave, I buried my nose in the soft top-knot between his ears and drew in his smell. I always thought he smelled so sweet there, and I knew I would never smell that sweetness again. A river rock reads, "Pepper 1977-1992." On the porch near his grave I have hung wind chimes, masses of tiny, golden bells that tinkle softly when the wind blows. When I hear them, I think, "Listen, Pepper, there's music for you."

Americans are peculiar about death. Bodies are whisked away out of hospital beds, hidden in false compartments under special carts so that no one confronts death face on. We no longer prepare the dead, but leave them to the care of strangers skilled at making the dead look like they are merely napping. Some people even choose to be foil-wrapped after death and stored in freezers with the hope that they can be restored to life when technology finally "defeats" death once and for all.

Yet all of nature reminds us that death is a necessary step along the trail of life. Death creates the arena for new life and growth, as we experience death and rebirth in each season. In our hearts and minds, old ideas die away making room for the new. In the physical world, all that "becomes" on earth is a rich composite of the decay, the rejoining, the creative assembly, of particles and elements that have always been a part of our universe. In a very real sense, we are the stuff of star dust and dinosaurs. Returning to the earth mother whose elements have created and sustained our bodies is as natural a process as birth itself.

When I was first diagnosed with cancer, my best friend gave me a gift. She told me that if I wanted to live, she would support me in any way possible, and if I wanted to die, that was okay with her, too. She said, "Susan, sometimes I'm tired of being here myself, and if your spirit is ready to leave, I won't argue with you about staying here." She was letting me choose, and respecting my choice. No one in the course of my illness

PHOTO: SUMNER W. FOWLER

offered me a greater or more loving gift. When I perceived death as a choice, albeit not necessarily a conscious one, a good deal of my fear evaporated. Perhaps I was ready to choose death in some way I didn't yet understand. And perhaps, just possibly, it would be okay to die. Or okay to live. Choice, the greatest gift of all.

With the medical technology available to us and to our animals today, respecting that a living being may choose to die is a lesson many of us have yet to learn. In my hospice work I watched certain families cling desperately to their cancer-ravaged loved ones, even when death was desired by the sufferer. "Hold on," we cry, "don't go!" And our loved ones struggle to stay for our benefit, not theirs. We do this with our animals as well, assuming that they would rather stumble blindly behind us in old age, bent with arthritis, deaf to our calls, riddled with infections and lumps, unable to feed or relieve themselves without our help. Some animals, I believe, would rather stay. But some would not. We must learn to hear them and respect their choice.

Tina Hodge and her family run a wildlife rehabilitation center in a small town in California. The animals there have offered some provocative lessons about death and choice. Tina's miraculous stories led me to a new level of awareness about respecting life and death.

As we watched the spotted fawn lick the ears of the sleeping wolf, the warden signed our Wild Animal Rehabilitation license. Thus began the procession of injured animals into our lives. Many of these creatures did not live. Fortunately, a large number of successful recoveries accompanied what we thought at the time were our "failures."

After ten years of this work, a most special bird came to teach us a strong and necessary lesson. It was an Arctic Loon. Some people down on the beach had seen the bird unable to walk, and had captured it. We thought maybe the rescuers had acted too hastily. These seabirds spend much of their time on the open water and very little time on shore. Their legs are awkward at best for land travel, and we decided it was best to put the loon in a tub of water, feed it, and return it to the ocean the next day. We brought the loon some fish and settled down to watch this amazing bird that can dive two hundred feet down in the sea to catch its prey. The loon was swimming about alert and active, and all seemed well.

Then the dance began. The loon's neck arched completely back, then came about in a slow circle, then stretched forward as its wings reached out and back. The dance, in perfect rhythm to some silent song, continued on as we sat mesmerized and time stood still. Words fail to convey what was being communicated to us two human witnesses. After the loon had died and its spirit had left, we turned to each other and saw the tears and joy gleaming from our eyes.

The loon's dance brought us the gift of understanding the beauty and joy of death. We were changed. We no longer could view death as a failure. The animals that come to us to die are allowing us a great intimacy. The loon taught us that it is an honor to assist in the process of crossing over. We stopped trying to prevent death when that path is chosen. In sixteen years, we have used euthanasia twice: Once for a great horned owl who was hit by an airplane, and once for a dog who had a very long series of seizures. We feel that suffering, struggle, and pain are all part of our journey within these bodies. The process is not something to be avoided but, rather, something to be experienced and completed so the soul can move on to other lessons.

Over the years, others have come to guide us in this sacred work. A Native American medicine woman shared with us her work with dying people. Her information has been of great help in assisting us with the death of both animals and people. At her suggestion, we now ask the animal or person leaving to take a message to God or to the Great Spirit on our behalf. This request gives the soul a purpose and helps it look forward to its journey, rather than looking back and resisting the transition. The correct message comes to us at the appropriate time. It can be as simple as "Please send help for the animals," or "Please guide us to peace on earth."

In our work, we have learned to seek healing permission from both the Creator (God, Great Spirit, whatever) and from the animal in question. If permission is not granted from both—and we rely deeply on our instincts and inner voice for guidance—we stop trying to support life and begin assisting in the death process.

As the body loosens its hold on the spirit, we begin the Death Chant:

Never the spirit was born.
The spirit shall cease to be never.
Never was time.
It was not.
Ending and beginning are dreams.
Birthless and deathless and changeless
Remain the spirit forever.
Death has not touched her at all.
Death though the house of him seems.

We sing or say this chant at least four times. It is meant to help the spirit in crossing over, but we've found it helps keep things in perspective for those helping out on this side as well. We are the visible helpers in this remarkable process, but we are not alone in our efforts. Beings of light and love are welcoming the spirit from their side. We trust our education will continue.

Rita Reynolds has devoted much of her time to supporting animals through the death process in a similar, but slightly different manner. She has committed herself to taking on elderly animal companions and opening her home to them in their last months of life. In addition, she publishes a wonderful magazine call *laJoie*, which is a bi-monthly collection of stories that celebrate animals and our special relationships with them. Writes Rita:

During the past decade, quite without distress or effort, I have found myself drawn with increasing frequency both to elderly animals and to animals in their last stages of life. With remarkable insight and centeredness, the life/death transition process began opening up for me, first through animals in my own family, and then with those living in other homes. With overwhelming respect, honor, and awe, I have been able to assist constructively in this process.

Three years ago, I began letting other people know that I was available to help people work with the death transition of their animal companions. In May 1994, my vet asked if I could help find a home for his ailing parents' thirteen-year-old Golden Retriever, Penny. We already had thirteen of our own dogs at home. But after following my instincts, I realized that Penny was to come live with us—live out the rest of her life with our large family of humans, canines, felines, and other assorted creatures. Somehow, I just felt that this was all part of some enormous, magnificent plan. And I looked forward to Penny's coming with expectation and joy.

Penny came to live with us three weeks later. She brought with her many excellent attributes that helped her adjust to life in her new home, attributes I had forgotten to express in my own life, such as facing change with a sense of adventure, the importance of playfulness no matter one's age, the profound delight in bringing people together to fulfill mutual needs. Because of Penny's age, these qualities seemed to shine in her with added brightness.

For the first time in thirteen years, Penny learned how to climb stairs. She discovered cats, an endless pleasure for her. She would watch them, chase them, bathe them ever-so-gently with her tongue, and speak to them with resounding, "wuf wufs" that were, like the tongue baths, so gentle around the edges. She learned about alpha dogs and packs, all new to one who had been an only dog all those previous years.

But it was her passing in February of that next year that brought the greatest insights to me. Barely with us six months, Penny had become much more than familiar to us. It was as though some ancient sage dwelled in that massive, golden frame, and I felt as though she had lived with us forever. Then one evening, she simply collapsed and shortly after died of inoperable cancer. In moving through my grief, I followed the steps I had outlined to others so many times before. I sat in silence. I sent loving supportive messages to her. I spoke aloud to her, sensing that whatever plane she was on, she would hear and appreciate my words. I wrote in detail about all that she had reminded me of, all that she had taught me.

Without question, I knew that I would maintain an ever-open door in my heart and home for other elder animals in need of love and assistance in their final days. I made such a pledge to Penny, to all of life, right out loud and standing in the middle of my living room floor, and I meant every word. So we do, indeed, have choice. Writer Barry Lopez says, "When you really want to have wisdom, open all the doors, and listen."

Our relationships with animal companions do not need to end with death. Animals may come back to us in some manner. And some animals seem to have an unusual sense of their departed human companions. Our companion animals sometimes return in dreams or in conscious visions. To me, these visits testify to an everlasting bond of love. Barbara Buschegger and her dog Sheba have met several times since Sheba's death. What is particularly unusual about Barbara's story is that other family members have seen Sheba, too.

I wanted to bury her in the yard, so I went to the vet hospital to bring her home. When I got home, the phone was ringing, so I left Sheba's body in the car and ran in to answer it. I got about five calls in a row, all from friends concerned about Sheba. I finally got up to return the phone to its cradle, and when I turned down the hall, I saw Sheba walking through the kitchen toward me. I couldn't believe my eyes. I rubbed them and rubbed them, and when I opened them she was gone. It wasn't like looking at a healthy, living animal, but more like looking at a transparency. I believe all things and beings have souls and what I saw was Sheba's soul coming back home.

In April, some of our family went to our cabin for the weekend. When they came back, my cousin's wife said, "Your dog paid us a visit." She said Sheba paid my sister-in-law a visit as well. When I asked what happened, she said Sheba was sitting by the cabin bunk when she came in. Sheba sat there for a long, long time just watching her until she shooed her away.

When I told my friend Maureen Michelson about this amazing story, she had a remarkable story of her own. Their old dog, Buddy, died two years ago, and Maureen's family had recently acquired two young puppies. Maureen and her five-year-old daughter Alexa were talking about death and how the spirit moves on after the person or animal dies. Maureen said,

"You can't see the spirits, but they ... " Alexa immediately interrupted her, emphatically stating, "Yes, you can see the spirits! When I let the puppies in the house sometimes Buddy comes in with them, and he told me he likes the puppies."

Sky, a white German Shepherd owned by Lee Hannon was the loving friend of Lee's father. The two visited many times during her father's long illness. Sky maintained an unexplainable connection to Lee's father after he died.

The day before my dad died, I brought Sky over to see him. Although my dad was bedridden, Sky still got a pat on the head and brought a smile to my dad's face. It was as if Sky sensed that it would be the last time he would ever see my dad. For the first time, Sky didn't jump up on the bed to get close to my father. Instead, he gave my father's hand a kiss and sat by his side.

Weeks later after my father died, I decided to take Sky with me to the cemetery. The ride there was almost bone-chilling: I said to Sky, "Do you want to see BaBa (our name for dad)?" and all of a sudden Sky started crying and barking and wagging his huge tail rapidly. We pulled into the parking space and before I was able to get my legs out of the car, Sky went running, pulling me behind him. He went directly to the wall of the mausoleum where my father lies. Sky jumped up on the wall and started scratching at it with his front paws. He was breathing so deeply that I started getting scared; but then I realized that he must be sensing my father in the wall. After awhile, Sky lay on the ground right under where my father rests. After about fifteen minutes I said, "Let's go, Sky," and with hesitation, Sky got up and went very slowly back to the car, glancing back a couple of times. He got in the backseat and laid down with a very solemn look. Since then, Sky and I go back to the cemetery every few weeks. Sky can't wait to get there, and he isn't quick to leave.

Sometimes the death of a pet is more about us, about our own limits and beliefs, than it is about partings. Laurie Lindquist wrote about her Elkhound, Signy, and the long and joyful time they had shared together. She also described Signy's increasing age and infirmities and told of how Signy began biting children as her patience decreased and her discomfort rose proportionately. Laurie eventually made the painful decision to have Signy euthanized. She wrote, "My heart literally cracked as I turned away at the veterinarian's office, carrying Signy's collar, never looking back. There are moments in a life for which we cannot be reconciled, but to which we eventually must become adjusted. That was one such long moment."

Laurie's words struck me in a deep and painful place I also cannot reconcile. Not long ago, I made a decision to euthanize my wonderful orange tabby, Bear. He was my self-appointed singing bodyguard who followed me from room to room each day, honoring me with ear-splitting arias. Magnanimous in proportion to his great size, he welcomed every new creature, from chicks and rabbits to new kittens, into our household with delight and curious affection. Bear always had a funny thing about shoes and he would park all nineteen pounds of himself on any unsuspecting guest's feet and make great to-do over their shoes by hugging them close against his breast in ecstatic rapture. We used to joke that Bear had been a shoe salesman in his former life.

Perhaps due in part to his tremendous and uncanny empathy for the emotional ups and downs of our family, Bear had waged a long and rough war with recurring urinary blockages. He ideally required separate feeding and housing. His bladder attacks could come any time. During that last year, Bear had changed from a huge, laid-back, purring red butterball, to a crying, uncomfortable, pacing crank. In addition, he developed a strange neurological syndrome that would send the skin on his back rippling in irritating waves. Homeopathy didn't work. Nothing worked. My husband maintains an in-home office and his desk papers and catalogs all bore bloody urine stains as Bear announced his discomfort and displeasure.

With Bear's medical history, I could not imagine seeking another home for him. In the past, I had always taken pride in caring for my pets, no matter what it cost in time or money or energy to "fix" them. I had an image of myself as someone willing to invest any and all of my resources into my animals. Now I was married, and there were other family members and many other animal companions to consider, as well. Our financial resources as a family were finite, and we had spent literally thousands of dollars on Bear's medical care. Choices needed to be made. Bear had shoved me up against the heroic image of my own making, and I was beside myself with frustration and guilt.

On a cold evening in early January, Bear's sore bladder blocked up again. He approached me in the kitchen where I was preparing dinner, squatted on the floor, and meowed loudly as he strained to pass a few bloody dribbles. Through the haze of my own guilt and confusion, I will never know whether he was asking for help, or asking for release. I called the vet down the street. She came over with a syringe and a bottle and euthanized Bear as I rocked him gently in my lap. That night, I clipped a lock of Bear's silky orange hair, placing it in a lacquered green box where a curl of Keesha's fur remains. I placed Bear in a cardboard box with his collar and old toys, and sobbed for hours. Nightmares assailed me when I finally went to bed.

The woman who buried Bear under an old pussy willow tree the next morning was not the woman I had believed myself to be. I wasn't all powerful, I wasn't all-sacrificing, and I wasn't heroic. The woman who buried Bear was someone with limits, with needs, with boundaries. She was someone Bear introduced me to, someone I hope Bear knew I needed to meet. I don't know to this day if the choice I made was the right one, but I have learned to live with the uneasiness of uncertainty.

Stories and lessons about death and final passages continue to fill my mailbox. The more I learn from animals about death, the more I realize that my experiences merely scratch the surface of a concept I can only rudimentarily grasp. There is so much love, life, and learning within the encompassing sphere of our leavetaking that I am left to wonder—with humility, awe, and a certain amount of respectful terror—what comes next?

▲ ▲ ▲

Vigil of the Cemetery Dog

My seventeen-year-old son was killed in a diving accident. Only a parent who has lost a child can understand the personal devastation. The evening before the accident, I happened to drive by our local cemetery. Sitting next to the fence was a stray dog. She sat on a small knoll between two trees, seemingly waiting for someone. She looked like a bedraggled red fox. Little did I know that three days later I would be burying my son on the exact spot where the little dog waited.

On the day of my son's funeral service, I saw the little dog again. She was standing a short distance away from where we gathered at the cemetery. The next morning, just before dawn, I went to visit my son's grave for the first time. And sitting beside the mound of flowers at his graveside was the little red dog. As I approached, she rose and stepped back a few feet, as if in respect. When I sat on the ground by the grave, she came back and sat beside me, not touching me or asking for attention for herself. She seemed to just "be there" for me. Together we watched the sun rise, and I felt a slight touch of peace. I arose and she walked me back to my car, then returned to my son's grave and lay down on it. The next morning was a repeat of the first. There she was, nestled beside the flowers. As she sat beside me, I ran my hand down along her back. She was slightly wet, as if from night dew. "You been here all night?" I asked. She answered with a slight wag of her tail. "What are you? Some kind of a guardian angel?" She turned toward me and looked at me with eyes that seemed to reach my very soul. I began to cry and tell her of my terrible pain, and she sat and listened.

The next morning, there she was. Beginning to think of someone besides myself, I had brought a bowl of food and some water for her. Apparently someone else had noticed that the little dog was doing twenty-four-hour duty, because there was a bowl of water by the grave. Knowing that my son wasn't alone, that he had this small dog with him, began to give me comfort. I remembered that several years before, my son and a friend had rescued a small red dog that had been shot with an arrow. My son named her Callie, and she stayed on as a beloved pet until an untimely accident took her life.

After about a week, I took the cemetery dog home with me. Strangely enough, she was quiet and subdued. I couldn't think of a name for her. Then one day, I said, "You know something? You look just like old Callie." It was as if I'd hit a magic switch. "Callie" stood up and, tail wagging furiously, ran over to me and put her paw up on my knee. It was as if she had finally "come home."

Who is this dog who showed me my son's cemetery plot, and then did round-the-clock sentry duty when my son was laid to rest there? Who is this dog who was there to help me through the greatest trauma of my life, who now shares my home and helps fill the lonely moments? Is there such a thing as reincarnation, and are dogs reincarnated? I don't know. I just know that she came into my life in a very mysterious way. My other dogs couldn't give me the comfort that this little red dog did, and still does.

Callie

PHOTO: DORIS MITCHELL

Callie has since become TDI (Therapy Dogs International)-certified. I take her on regular visits to our local nursing home where she has become the "adopted dog." I am very proud of Callie. During the days following the Oklahoma bombing, TDI-certified dogs—including my Callie—were taken to the rescue center and to the church where the victims' families were waiting. Callie, with her gentle way, made many friends. In an especially touching moment, a medical worker sat on the floor with her arms around Callie, petting her and sharing her personal pain. It reminded me of myself as I sat with Callie at my son's grave only last June. I'd never thought one way or another about angels or guardians but now I know there is such a thing.

—*Doris Mitchell*

Sadie's Tear

When my mother was close to death, the hospital removed all mechanical equipment and withheld food and drink as she was in a coma. I went up to see her the evening that she died. My brother and his wife had left about an hour before. I entered the cold, dark, private room that was off in a hospital corner by itself. This moment was the closest I'd ever been to death, and it was eerie. I asked the nurses for a blanket for my mother and they didn't seem concerned or eager to please. I tried talking to my mother while I listened to her horrible gasping. Her lips were so parched I went into the bathroom to get some water for her and began putting droplets of water in her mouth and on her lips.

A tear rolled down from her left eye. That tear bothered me for a long time. I kept wondering if my brother and wife had said something painful in front of my mother without realizing that she could perhaps still hear. She died that evening and the reason behind the tear angered and frustrated me for a long time afterward.

One day my husband brought home an old raggedy dog that had been abandoned by some renters. We named her Sadie. It was evident that she was quite elderly and had bad arthritis and some unknown problem with her stomach. One of our vets decided to operate on her as her stomach condition deteriorated. Though we brought her home and pampered her, her health worsened.

One night she collapsed on the kitchen floor. I rested her head on my leg as I sat on the floor beside her and began putting tiny pieces of food and droplets of water into her mouth. As I looked down at her, I suddenly saw one large tear spill out her left eye, just as I had witnessed at my mother's bedside. Instantly, the correlation was clear. The tear was a symbol of gratitude for an act of kindness. At long last, I had an answer to the question that had plagued me for almost a year. Sadie passed away within that next week. I had wished so often that my mother could have told me why she cried that tear, and I felt that through Sadie, she had.

—*Jeanette Schmitt*

Letting Go

During the last week of our dog Max's life, he was in tremendous pain and would have tremors or shudders of sadness. I wanted to have him put to sleep, but my husband insisted we wait until he returned home from a trip so we could make the decision together. So the children and I waited the week out, and I had an insightful moment with Max one morning. His eyes told me that he was enduring and holding on because he sensed our fear of losing him. As I stroked his fur, I told him that he didn't have to be strong for me anymore, that I was willing to let him go, and that I'd be okay without him because I'd take him with me in my memory. Then I explained all this to our teenage girls and encouraged them to find a quiet moment to have a similar talk with Max, their canine sibling. My husband finally came home on Thursday night, and we all had an evening to be home together as a family. We were planning to have Max put down the next day, but Friday morning when we woke up, Max had died. We cried harder that day for Max than we had at Grandpa's funeral, which really surprised us. But then we realized that our expressions for Max were less encumbered than our feelings had been at a formal human service.

—*Melinda Paterson*

Waiting to Rise

As a child, I believed
if I opened my window at night
the darkness would disappear . . .

Today, at five in the afternoon,
I love him suddenly.
A hardened paw print, like a fossil,
on the dirt drive reminds me.

We buried him last night under the orange trees
because he likes the shade.
With the full moon and a flashlight
I watched my daughter grow lovely,
a small mound of moist earth
she strained her slender muscles to dig.

A man, neither of us knew then,
wiped perspiration from his face and eyes.
His back glistened in the pale light.
While his pick loosened the dirt and rocks;
my daughter, solemn-faced and determined,
shoveled.

I don't know if remembering him now
is an act of despair or an apology
I invent to make him stay.
Sudden love is like that.

While he, his print firmly on our drive,
is ready to be without love—
as I am not—ready to disappear.

His heart must have become light
like a white balloon—soaring
out of our reach towards heaven.
His body left stiff in the wheelbarrow,
plastic bags covering a fur still warm.

Maybe this is all possible—
but I am older now.
Still, maybe it happened to this Shepherd,
While the moon hung loosely in the black sky
waiting for a window.
Waiting to rise.

—*Susan Clayton-Golder*

Winnie

Our fine and excellent little friend—whom we call Winnie—
has been gone three days now. I last spoke to her on Thanksgiving morning and there was no doubt in my mind that the
loss of her tailfeathers and the terrific cold had laid her low.
She remained near the ground on a branch waiting for her
meal, peering at me with a quiet exhaustion that in retrospect
was a prayer for help, a half-breath in the wilderness. And so I
thought to pick her up and take her indoors, this mystery of

creation who had so blessed and animated our garden for three months.

She had arrived one summer morning out of the unaccountable yonder from the Vietnamese highlands—we were later to learn—a species of Laughing Thrush thought to be extinct. She looked like an overgrown baby Chinstrap Penguin with a lemon breast. Winnie spoke in a frenzy of phonemes and sibilants, defended her new-found turf with Falstaffian joviality, befriended squirrels, cried out to Blue Jays, and closely inspected my wife and me who fed her religiously three times a day. Her meals consisted of chopped fruits, nuts, occasional cat food, and fresh white corn. We set up an elaborate gazebo with heat lamps and tropical trees and perches to complement her wild exterior landscape.

We welcomed her as visiting royalty to this country, unable to divine her unlikely origins. For three months, her unceasing joy and presence brought the garden fantastically alive in new ways. Winnie truly touched the lives of all the many creatures—birds, possums, mice, rats, squirrels—who frequent our home. The effects were palpable, we could see it. To gaze at Winnie was to know the meaning of wilderness, which is Love. Love unremitting: The love that John Muir commented on when he watched grizzly bears loping; the love that emanates from someone like His Holiness the Dalai Lama as he dignifies each and everyone of those he meets; love which is the compassion enshrined in the vision of Mahavira, most recent sage of Jainism, a mortal man who walked naked for forty-two years throughout India preaching *ahimsa*—

nonviolence—and speaking with the animals. Or the abiding love of St. Francis for wolves and pigeons.

I see Winnie in her homeland, eternally, prancing about the great Buddist temple complexes—Ninh-phuc, Van-phuc, Thien-phuc—their carved stoneworks fashioned with teardrops and dragons. Spirits hovering about the full moons of ancient highlands, and Winnie sleeping starbound in her hutch of golden grains.

We loved her so. Why I did not bring her temporarily indoors will remain with me always—the essence of implacable guilt and bad-timing. She had been suffering in her new North American adventure, though she scarcely let on. It was too cold in Southern California around Thanksgiving. There were too many hawks and cats, and our lavish meals for her were probably not appropriate, though her eating habits suggested a full, voracious subscription to our gourmet preparations. I had planned to bring Winnie in after we returned from our Thanksgiving dinner visit with a close friend, and to nurse her back to her "old" self. It was all a question of three hours.

But, alas, there is no doubt about it: she is gone. The lesson: never celebrate Thanksgiving unless you have truly "given." The world's animals are in such peril because of us that a lifetime of due-diligence on behalf of the earth's living beings is the only acceptable corollary and prelude to a truly human life. There is a reason we are here. A purpose that has the recommendations of nearly four billion years of evolutionary experimentation behind it. That purpose is consciousness—our capacity to engender a "new nature," to become islands of consciousness in a sea of evolutionary tumult. We are to reach out, however awkward and groping our attempts, and bring love to other species. If we fail, our epitaph shall read, "The shortest lived species in the annals of biology." The only alternative to that epitaph is constant, dedicated sharing; partnership with all creatures. Winnie made that partnership so abundantly clear. She was a genius of social graces, of tact and companionship. How can I convey the miracle of her to you? If she harbored a message, it was this: be graceful, be loving, be compassionate. That is the essence of life.

I am galled and chilled and mortified that, in spite of our overflowing love for her, we were incapable of protecting Winnie. Every "parent" feels this discrepancy between the dictates of logic and love, and the utter exasperation and uncontrollability of reality. That we felt like parents to Winnie is, perhaps, the keenest insight I can suggest: Winnie had elicited profound interspecies altruism in two ungainly, bipedal mammals whose combined weight must have exceeded hers by eight hundred times.

I don't know where Winnie is. I pray that if by chance she's headed South, she finds eternal peace. I dedicate myself to her perfect mystery and majesty. The world—God, nature, every ideal—could never achieve any greater truth than she who shall remain inside us.

—*Michael Tobias and Jane Morrison*

The River of Horses

I look into the dark pools
of the pony's eyes.
Her pain has distanced her from me—
as if she is looking up from some deep canyon.

I wait for the vet to come
press my forehead to her sweet, suffering face.
My human tears, the only comfort I can offer,
break loose from clenched eyelids
to wet the rough hair of her cheek.

From the depths of her pain
I hear a far-away thunder.
Like white water rushing wildly
through a deeply cut arroyo.

What I hear is not water
but resounding hoofbeats—
a stream of countless galloping horses
sharing the exaltation of their one fluid soul.

It is a river of horses.
Calling the pony to join them.
Offering her rightful place among them.
Washing away her pain with their joy.

We pull the pony back.
To the vet's needles in an occluded vein
to the aching calls of a small girl-child who
loves her beyond the measure of all tears.

In her eyes I still see the river of horses
yet she forgives us our guilty love
our clumsy attempts to save her life.

She stays to teach the child.
To trust that what we no longer see still exists.
To know a wholeness greater than pain.
To understand that sometimes
the most loving embrace is an open hand.

I stretch my arms to hold
a pain beyond my reach.
I watch, with an ache in my womb,
as child-soul is made tender and open
by a pony's terrible need to die.

The child, guided only
by a communion of deep animal-knowing,
learns to first touch that compassionate knife
    to her own breast
helps her friend to cross unseen waters, alone.

The pony looks back at the child
blesses the living with soft eyes
and goes to take her place in the river of horses.
Set free through a hole in a little girl's heart.

—*Ronni Sweet*

PHOTO: NATIONAL ARCHIVES, YELLOWSTONE NATIONAL PARK

CHAPTER SEVEN

The Wolf:

ANIMALS AS MYTH AND SYMBOL

In the wolf, we have not so much an animal that we have always known as one that we have consistently imagined. We embark then on an observation of an imaginary creature, not in the pejorative but in the enlightened sense—a wolf from which all other wolves are derived. Joseph Campbell ... wrote ... that men do not discover their gods, they create them. So do they also, I thought, create their animals.

—BARRY LOPEZ
Of Wolves and Men

Certain animals have attained an historic stature that far transcends their biological reality. They are the animals of legend, myth, and symbol. They are animals we project ourselves upon, who become a metaphor for qualities we desire or despise. Our perception of these animals can expand far beyond the realm of the physical. Many cultures and societies have imbued certain animals with fantastically lofty or hellish characteristics, and have handed down their beliefs to subsequent generations through art, literature, and oral tradition. Some of our notions about "bad," "noble," "useful," "conniving," and "dangerous" animals seem so firmly rooted in our cultural consciousness that we have become blind to the fact that these are qualities we have invented, defined, and bestowed upon them without thought to the consequences for the animals or for us. We have held these mental pictures for so long that we forget to question them. These assumptions, which eventually become legendary, have much to teach—not about the animals, but about us.

The attributes I attach to various animals illuminate values and beliefs that define who I am. And as a nation, the animals we symbolically embrace or despise help to define our collective spirit at any given moment in history. How an animal becomes a symbol, or a stereotype depends on the circumstances, fears, desires, and prejudices of a particular people and time in history.

The lessons animals bring us as a community lie in our willingness first to acknowledge, then to question, our historic and current attitudes towards them. Why have certain animals been defined as "varmints"? Why have we collectively decided it is acceptable to kill "nuisance" animals? Why do we accept extinction for certain animals, yet protect others? If myths tell us that all predatory animals are cruel and merciless, how do we feel about ourselves, the supreme predators? Mythologist Joseph Campbell has written that as our old myths become outdated and stale in the passage of the ages, we must create new and viable myths to carry us forward. We need myths that can speak to our children of love, compassion, mercy, and courage.

As symbol, there are many examples of animals who represent both good and evil. Depending on the community, culture, or country, a particular animal may be both loved and despised. And even within a community, depending on one's political or religious beliefs, a certain animal may be considered friend or foe. For example, in the Judeo-Christian tradition, snakes represent the fall of Adam and Eve and are considered evil. However, among many Native American tribes, the snake embodies the power of transmutation and creation.

We continue to create animals as symbols to represent the conflicts of our times. In the Pacific Northwest, there is a small but powerful animal that has taken on mythological proportions as a symbol for a fierce conflict between the logging industry and environmentalists. The spotted owl has recently become an international symbol of destruction and extinction. For environmentalists, the precarious future of the spotted owl represents the death of our nation's last old-growth forests, as well as the death of the spotted owl and many other species who thrive there. For loggers, the owl symbolizes the end of their livelihood, towns and industry, and a way of life that thrived in some families for generations. While environmentalists produce beautiful posters of spotted owls perched in ancient trees, loggers sport bumper stickers that proclaim, "Shoot an owl, save a logger." Unfortunately, the Northwest is faced with additional conflicts over the environment, in particular, the management of its rivers. The salmon now stand side-by-side with the spotted owl as a symbol of the ongoing struggle to determine how the environment will be managed, and what economic sacrifices the public will consider acceptable or unacceptable.

One animal in particular has captured the human imagination since the beginning of recorded history—the wolf. Most cultures, religions, and countries worldwide have singled out the wolf as a symbol of enormous good or devastating evil. In my search for myths and legends about the wolf, I was amazed at the sheer magnitude of information available. One book in particular, *Of Wolves and Men*, by Barry Lopez, is a virtual wolf bible, and his research has influenced my thinking considerably. What surfaced repeatedly was a mythic vision of the dual nature of the wolf. Wolves embody both masculine and feminine aspects, since the wolf is considered both gifted parent (the feminine) and fierce hunter (the masculine). Because wolves see well in both day and night, they are considered a crossover animal representing both light and dark. In fact, the Greek words for "wolf" and for "light" are so closely associated that there is some confusion over whether Apollo was a wolf god or a sun god, or both. Over and over again the wolf is referred to as the twilight hunter, inhabiting the realms of shadow just before dark, just before dawn. The wolf also represents the guardian of the gates of heaven or hell. The wolf is associated with the dual roles of destroyer and provider. When it destroys a life to survive, the killing provides nourishment not only for the wolf pack, but also for many hungry birds, animals, and insects who depend on the remains.

The Wolf

Wolves are historically credited with caring for lost children who sometimes grow up to become legendary heroes and leaders. On the other hand, wolves have been cursed for killing lost travelers.

In distilling the legends into a simple framework, the wolf can be seen as almost universally representing light or dark, and the space between. Dr. Elizabeth Kirkhart, a Jungian psychologist with a special interest in archetypal images and symbols, agrees that wolves represent a transitional or crossover spirit.

In many cultures, the wolf appears as a psychopomp, a figure that acts as a mediator between the ego and the unconscious, between death and transformation. Historically, we have over-identified with the dark side of the wolf. But the wolf is not just one or the other. It moves between and throughout *both* realms. It embodies the light and the shadow. Many people are afraid to confront what we call "the shadow," those uncomfortable and unclaimed aspects and urges within us that we find primitive, deadly, and shameful. We look for a target, someplace to project all the self-hatred or shame we carry inside. Throughout history, wolves have served as such a target.

No one seems eager to confront and make peace with the wild wolf lurking around inside each of us. It is easier to despise our projection than to do the personal work necessary to integrate our own inner dark wolf. But unless we can face and claim the dark aspects of the wolf, we are not free to enjoy the light aspects: the courage, intelligence, and fierce joy of living that the wolf also embodies. This is the wolf's challenge to us: to embrace it all.

The earliest roots of the mythical wolf can be traced to Stone Age hunters. They were the first to bestow positive qualities on the wolf, respecting the wolf as a skilled and enduring hunter, community provider, then hunting companion, and later as hearth-mate or dog as the progeny of wolves became one of our first domesticated animals.

But as hunters and gatherers became shepherds and farmers, the mythic wolf's positive attributes faded. Wolves could destroy a family's complete livelihood—a small flock of sheep or goats—in one night. The threat of the biological wolf on small farming communities was very real. However, from a more spiritual or psychological perspective, as humans struggled with the trappings of agri-based, civilized life, primitive urges became increasingly shameful in the new social order. Wildness in any form was not seen as a virtue, but rather some old, scary afterthought from a beastly time in humanity's past. Wolves became a dramatic symbol and a frightening reminder of wildness and uncontrollable primitiveness. During medieval times and throughout the dark history of the Inquisition, as people fought with the conflicting concepts of civilization and witchcraft, of sin and heavenly redemption, men and women were accused in epidemic proportions of being werewolves. These were demonic creatures who symbolized people falling to their lowest and most depraved natures. Barry Lopez describes this hideous wolf-related phenomenon in *Of Wolves and Men*.

In a hunter society, traits that were universally admired—courage, hunting skill, endurance—placed the wolf in a pantheon of respected animals; but when man turned to agriculture and husbandry, to cities, the very same wolf was hated ... The wolf remains unchanged but man now speaks of his hated "animal" nature. By standing around a burning stake, jeering at and cursing an accused werewolf, a person demonstrated an allegiance to his human nature and increased his own sense of well-being. The tragedy ... is that the projection of such self-hatred was never satisfied. No amount of carnage, no pile of wolves in the village square, was enough to end it.

It is fascinating to note that bears and wild cats were equal threats to the first shepherds and a far greater menace to humans, but they never assumed the level of loathing European herdsmen and villagers bestowed upon the wolf. Why they didn't is still subject for heated discussion. It is postulated, though, that wolves are far more like humans in habit than bears, big cats, or other wild dogs such as coyotes and foxes. Of these animals, only wolves are social animals who live and hunt in close family units and mate for life. In addition, through our beloved dogs, we have an ancient link with wolves unlike any we have with other animals.

The wolf's association with the demonic began in the early days of Christianity when the new Christians appointed the image of the pure, gentle lamb for Christ and other martyrs. The lamb-devouring wolf then became the symbol of the devil—slaughterer of God's lambs. An ivory carving from 900 AD depicts Christ on the cross, a snarling wolf below. Thus the wolf was chained to Satan for hundreds of years through religious art, hymn, and legend.

Barry Lopez writes of a later and even more devastating chapter in the history of humans and wolves that helped plant the seeds for the eventual wholesale slaughter of wolves on our continent. In the 1600s, philosopher René Descartes articulated the belief that animals had no souls, were essentially living machines, and were put on earth specifically for human use. Therefore, according to Descartes, humans need not feel guilty about killing animals, because such killing bore no moral consequences. This belief was enthusiastically embraced by the Catholic Church, then busy denouncing paganism. Paganism in general held that animals had spirits, did not belong to humans, and should not be thoughtlessly killed.

The power of Cartesian logic both then and now cannot be overestimated. It still flourishes today and has invaded all of our sciences and many of our religious traditions with a distorted sense of self-importance and universal lordship over a "soul-less planet." Cartesian logic substantiates the Christian interpretation of human domination, rather than stewardship, of the earth and all its beings. It has served as the green light for the slaughter and extinction of countless species. And it paved the way for the remorseless massacre and brutal torture of thousands, perhaps even millions, of wolves in America in the late nineteenth and early twentieth centuries.

The America that confronted the settlers of the 1700s was a vast, enormous wilderness of dense towering forests, and unknown and innumerable dangers. Pilgrim settlers were terrified at the fearsome size and incomprehensibility of the wilderness that surrounded them. The wolf and its haunting trademark howl was quickly targeted as a symbol of wild chaos, primitive drives, and enormous appetite—all notions inherently evil to a tiny band of European foreigners desperate for stability, restraint, and domestication. Puritan leader Cotton Mather wrote, "What is not useful is vicious." Another early settler wrote, "One of the most noxious of all our animals is the wolf. When a number of them associate it is not for peace but for war and destruction." This Puritan view of the wilderness and the wolf prevailed in America for the next two hundred years.

With the moral and historical justification of a wilderness that needed taming, and righteous biblical vengeance against the "beast of waste and desolation," as Theodore Roosevelt later baptized the wolf, Americans began slaughtering wolves in an extensive predator-control campaign. The destruction of the wolf in America in the nineteenth and twentieth centuries would reach an unprecedented scale. Eric Zimen, a wolf biologist from Germany, dumbfounded at the magnitude and viciousness of the slaughter said, "We killed the wolf in Europe, and we hated the wolf, but it was not anything like what you have done in America."

Americans killed other predators as well, but the slaughter of the wolf was unique in its excess and cruelty. Clearly, people were trying desperately to kill the mythic wolf as well as the living one. In an effort to wipe out the deep inner fear of our own inherent wildness, wolves were trapped, set on fire, and turned loose into dog packs after their jaws had been broken and their tendons sliced. They were poisoned with arsenic, strychnine, and cyanide in baiting programs that also killed millions of other creatures including birds, ferrets, hawks, eagles, squirrels, dogs, and children. For recreation, wolves were roped between two or three riders and dismembered alive. They were choked to death in snares. Pups were pulled from dens and burned alive or strangled. In the height of the wolf-killing mania, people even torched their own lands to destroy wolf habitat.

America's nineteenth-century ranching community carried the wolf wars to a greater and even more destructive level. Land was scarce, foreign-investor money was drying up, and water rights had become an issue. Disease and weather took their toll on livestock. Cattle prices fluctuated. As Native Americans were forced onto reservations, the wolf was the only symbolic target left for the long, downhill slide of the livestock industry that had reached and surpassed its Montana heyday in the mid-1880s. In 1931, at the loud urging of a fanatical ranching minority, the federal government passed its infamous Eradication and Control of Predatory and Other Wild Animals Act, which is still in effect today. Although control of the weather and the economy remained impossible, ranchers could always take their frustrations out on the wolf, and they did so with a vengeance and with government assistance.

Historian Edward Curnow writes that the ranchers grew to view the dwindling wolf as "an object of pathological hatred." Although a sudden hail storm could kill more livestock in an hour than wolves would kill in a year, the slaughter and torture of wolves continued long after wolves were a threat to anyone. Except for a small population of wolves in Min-

Susan McElroy met her first wolf in 1981.

PHOTO: BARBARA MELVILLE

nesota, by 1945 virtually no wolves remained in the continental states.

In the ranching community today, hatred for the wolf is still strong, a sentiment I find difficult to comprehend. I wanted answers, so I brought my questions to my friend and former husband. Bill is an Idaho native from a strong ranching background who was once himself a trapper of predators. Bill's father was a government predator-control hunter, and his cousin still traps for the government. If anyone could answer my questions honestly about wolf hatred from the perspective of a rancher, a trapper, a hunter, it is Bill. "Why all the hatred?" I asked him. "Why all the frenzy about livestock being slaughtered and the big game going away? Wasn't there plenty of big game when the first settlers arrived and wolves were thick in virtually every part of the continent? Aren't wolves and ranchers coexisting in Minnesota and Canada?"

"It's fear," Bill answered simply and honestly. "Just about none of the ranchers around here have ever seen a wolf. My dad never saw one—they were all dead by the time he took up trapping. It's the stories, handed down for a hundred years. Stories about animals that are huge and strong and smart. It wasn't easy to get rid of them. But it's not so much even what wolves *do*. It's what a few wolves *could* do if they wanted to. And it's fear about more government control. Ranchers hate it when the government meddles in ranching business."

Bill's comments about fear corroborated my belief in the power of old myths and stories. But his last remark had surprised me because ranchers strongly depend on the government to keep them in business. Our government kills predators at the demand of ranchers. By charging ranchers exceptionally low fees to use public lands for grazing, the U.S. government essentially subsidizes the ranching industry in one of America's largest entitlement programs. According to the magazine *Western Wildlands* (Fall/1989), almost ninety percent of Bureau of Land Management lands and sixty-nine percent of U.S. Forest Service lands are leased for grazing. Without these leases, the livestock industry claims it couldn't survive. So what was this aversion Bill described to government meddling and control? "How do you feel when you're heavily beholden to someone?" Bill asked. "When someone has that big a hand in your pocket?" And it suddenly made sense how the wolf could still be a target for the hostility and frustration that dependence engenders in anyone—in this case, the ranching community. It's easy to blame things outside of ourselves when we fear change. Again it was clear that the wolf issue had little to do with wolves.

It is only in the past few decades that Americans have begun to look at the wolf with something other than loathing. Even when we felt safe and civilized enough to embrace the concept of wilderness and create national parks in testimony to our new-found acceptance of the beauty and worth of the wild, there still remained the insistent, puritanical whisper of Cotton Mather to contend with: "What is not useful is vicious." Our national parks were established not as secure and permanent strongholds for wilderness or wildlife, but rather, according to official national park policy, for the "benefit and enjoyment of the people." In accordance with that doctrine, wolves and other predators have been systematically exterminated from our national parks.

In the course of researching this chapter, I visited Yellowstone National Park and met with some of the people coordinating Yellowstone's wolf recovery program. The recovery involves releasing several small groups of wild Canadian gray wolves into Yellowstone over the next five years. After more than twenty years of government planning, and in the face of intense public pressure both for and against the project, fourteen Canadian gray wolves were released in Yellowstone National Park in the winter of 1995. Some seventy years ago, wolves were systematically poisoned, trapped, and hunted out of existence. Now, they were being welcomed.

Wolf recovery has been a lifelong dream of mine. As the Yellowstone recovery plan became a reality, I felt compelled to explore more thoroughly the significance and symbolism of the wolf and its landmark return. I wanted to understand what this program signified for the country, as well as what it meant for me personally. In my cancer visualizations, I had invested my imaginary wolves with tremendous import. Now, the wolves who had lived so fully in my mind were re-entering my life and the life of the nation in flesh and bone.

In my imaginings, the wolf brings lessons of health and power, joy of family, and the essence of "wild" creativity and spontaneity. That the wolf would return to Yellowstone—so close to my spiritual "home" of Jackson Hole—during the same year that this book was being created has enormous symbolic significance for me. The synchronicity of these two events is a reunion of heart and home, as though the universe were saying a great big "Yes!" as I worked toward the completion of the book.

Sam Woodring, chief ranger of Yellowstone in 1922, playing with eight wolf pups that were dug out of a den. Rangers shot the mother. A week later the pups were exterminated by order of park regulations to kill predatory animals.

PHOTO: NATIONAL ARCHIVES, YELLOWSTONE NATIONAL PARK

When I visited Yellowstone in the spring of 1995, wolves were once again singing in the woods of Yellowstone. Curious to learn more about the shared history of wolves and this national park, I spent time combing the park's archives. In particular, I wanted to find pictures of wolves in Yellowstone. I was told I wouldn't find many because there were few wolves left by the time the park was established in 1872. I found one photo, though, that haunted me. It was an old glass-plate negative of a man with two children playing with a litter of fat wolf pups. The man is Sam Woodring, then chief ranger of Yellowstone. He would go on to become the first superintendent of Grand Teton National Park. The photo looks innocent, the children and the pups carefree. Yet I was told that Woodring had killed the pups' parents and the pups in the photo were destroyed a few days later after their novelty had worn off, in accordance with park policy.

In the overflowing archival photo binders at Yellowstone, the contrasts in human consciousness seem to leap off the pages. Baby bears the size of a small shoebox, infant elk and antelope, tiny foxes and porcupine kits all suckle at bottles offered up by smiling park employees or visitors, or nestle securely in the willing laps of grownups and children. A page later, the adult versions of these animals are pictured in traps, as road kill, or lying dead alongside someone holding a rifle. The old photo images stamped indelibly on my mind are pages of black-and-white conflict, confusion, and age-old cruelty. The images portray a nation steeped in old myths and a biblical imperative to conquer, dominate, and subdue.

When I met with members of the wolf reintroduction

team, I had many questions. Some proponents had worked arduously for many years to return the wolf to Yellowstone. Had our national beliefs shifted in some way to allow the wolves to return? Did the recovery team members have any personal stories to share? What were the biggest obstacles facing the returning wolves?

I met one afternoon with Norm Bishop, Yellowstone resources interpreter. He compiles, interprets, and distributes the reams of literature about the Yellowstone wolf recovery plan. For every question I asked him, he had a documented answer. I already knew that the livestock industry was still vehemently opposed to the wolf's return to the park. I asked Norm what he believed their uproar was really all about, since a private group, Defenders of Wildlife, had promised full compensation to ranchers for any livestock lost to wolves. "It isn't about compensation," Norm responded. "It's about control of public lands, about change. People deeply fear change and loss of control. Because wolves go where they want and do what they want, they represent chaos or loss of order—our order, that is. We're not comfortable with chaos in our lives."

Eventually, I asked Norm what meaning the wolf had for him personally. He said, "Oh I'm very enthused about the reintroduction program." It was easy to see that he was, but I wanted to know why. He was silent for a moment before he finally answered, "Because we hurt so profoundly the things we don't understand." Then, he unraveled a story about a special dog he had owned many years before. It was "wolfish" in many of its manners, including its way of greeting, leaping up to nuzzle, lick, and nibble at his face. Norm said that sometimes his dog would accidentally catch the septum of his nose in these greetings, and it hurt. "I'd swat him away . . . hit him," he admitted. "Years later, when I first saw films of wolves greeting each other, it was like seeing my old dog. Have you ever seen wolves greet one another? They nose and push at each other's faces. Suddenly I realized that all that leaping and nibbling was his way of showing respect, devotion, love, honor, joy—all the good things I meant to him. And I hit him because I was hurt and annoyed and didn't understand. I wondered what it was like for him to be hit. It must have been utterly confusing to be so completely misunderstood." After sharing the story, Norm added, "I've always had an affinity for wolves and coyotes. I can't really tell you where it comes from. Just as I suspect that those who truly hate wolves can't really tell you where *that* comes from."

When I asked Mike Phillips, Wolf Project Leader, what he had learned from the wolves, Mike said, "Humility." Then he spoke of his respect for the recovery process, or restoration biology as it is called. Mike equates recovery with an act of creation or re-creation—bringing something back. "It wouldn't matter to me whether we were restoring wolves or mussels," Mike explained. "There's something deeply important about restoring anything. The complexity of recovery is humbling. And anything that helps us lose some of our human arrogance is a good thing."

I was also curious about the contemporary phenomenon of "wolf lovers." If our old myths about wolves had been so slanted to the dark, where had this shaft of light crept in? Who were the people who wanted the wolf back? Several members of the recovery team believe that the wolf represents the now beloved wilderness. We have proven that we can subdue the frontier, we have nothing more to fear. And as the fear subsides, Americans feel the aching loss of the wilderness as it disappears. There are no more dark corners in the forest. In an ironic twist of circumstance, the dark, chaotic, and uncontrollable places are now in our cities and streets. As though awakening from a centuries-long nightmare of domination and control, we long to reunite with the healing silence, freedom, and harmony of the wilderness. In his anthology, *Out Among the Wolves*, John Murray sums up this new shift in our perception of wolves.

> Humankind needs the wolf. We see in the wolf those values and traits without which we as a species will perish. A human being without a family, without roots, without work, a human being without a sense of place, of location, of community, is like a wolf without its pack, its home territory, its sense of belonging and purpose and security. The person becomes alienated, fearful, opportunistic, amoral, and, above all, alone. A society— or worse, a world—built of such people has lost its center, its heritage, and quite possibly determined its downfall. The wolf . . . reminds us of what we cannot forget: that our origins are out there, in the cold, windy outback of time, and that we are, despite all of the tinsel and trappings of civilization, still very much a part of that wild nature.

According to Rick Bass who has written extensively on wolves, two-thirds of the American population and up to ninety percent of visitors to national parks want the wolf returned to portions of the United States. Perhaps the American people want some things completely whole again. Less than a hundred years ago, the only wolf most Americans saw was on a bounty poster or a horror-movie advertisement. But in answer to public demand, wolves now decorate our calendars, paintings, clothes, wind chimes, kitchen towels, doormats, and greeting cards. Their jubilant voices ring out on tapes and CDs. Now, we are welcoming them back into our wilderness.

However, the sinister myths struggle to survive. As the wolves were released into Yellowstone, the Montana Farm Bureau Federation issued this bulletin: "Soon the killing will start. A little at first, then growing over time. Wildlife will diminish and hunting with it. Livestock will perish and ranches will go under. In twenty or thirty years, the wolf will reign supreme." Defying all scientific and historic evidence to the contrary proving that wolves can and do safely coexist with ranchers, hunters, and human communities around the world, these fears persist. An organization called the Abundant Wildlife Society publishes anti-wolf literature that is so extreme it would be funny if it weren't so vicious: "Wolves cannot be controlled, they kill and kill year-round. It is no wonder they have eliminated big game herds in parts of America....Wolves kill everything. They kill each other and every other kind of animal ... Wolves are of little *economic* [emphasis mine] value in comparison to [the] destruction it does to survive." If the word "wolves" was replaced with the word "humans" in this diatribe, these statements would ring true. What other animal in history has ever so clearly represented our dark side?

As I was finishing this chapter, an age-old, tragic, and eerily familiar scenario was being played out in Yellowstone. One of the fourteen wolves released in Yellowstone Park was a large, energetic male wolf known only as "Number Ten." Exploring outside the park boundary with his mate, he was shot and killed by a bear hunter. The hunter took the head and the skin of Number Ten, dumped his body into the brush, and tossed his radio collar into a stream. For an $11,000 bounty, a hunting partner turned him in to the authorities.

Canadian gray wolf, "Number Ten," was killed in 1995 by a hunter.

PHOTO: YELLOWSTONE NATIONAL PARK

When asked before television cameras why he had killed the wolf, the hunter simply remarked that he "liked to shoot things."

Number Ten's mate soon made news of her own. She gave birth to eight black pups in a shallow den near the site of Number Ten's murder. The squeaking pups were discovered by a biologist searching for the female's whereabouts. When I heard news of the birth, I thought again about the 1922 photo of the park ranger and the bundle of orphaned and trusting pups destroyed simply because they were wolves. This time, the story would end differently. This time, it would end with life. After much discussion, officials decided that the female wolf should be returned to Yellowstone Park where she could raise her young. Because there were no pack members or mate to help support and feed the wolf family, recovery team members would bring the wolf mother road kill until the young pups could hunt. The wolf pups and mother will be left in respectful seclusion to grow, and eventually will be released to thrive in the wilds of Yellowstone.

Perhaps the time has finally arrived for us to sit down and "take our place" at nature's table and share bread with the many animal nations already seated there for centuries without us. Perhaps the animals will forgive us our long absence and welcome us back. And perhaps they will rejoice that their lost brothers and sisters have at last returned to their souls' true home.

▲ ▲ ▲

Oh Great Spirit

In the name of Raven. In the name of Wolf. In the name of Whale.
Who have taught us. Who have guided us. Who have sustained us.
Who have healed us.

Please heal the animals.

In the name of Raven. In the name of Wolf. In the name of Whale. In the name of Snake. Whom we have slaughtered. Whom we have feared. Whom we have caged. Whom we have persecuted. Whom we have slandered. Whom we have cursed. Whom we have tortured.

Please protect the animals.

In the name of Raven. In the name of Wolf. In the name of Whale. In the name of Snake. Whose habitat we have stolen. Whose territory we have plundered. Whose feeding grounds we have paved or netted. Whose domain we have poisoned. Whose food we have appropriated. Whose young we have killed. Whose lives and ways of life we threaten.

Please restore the animals.

In the name of Raven. In the name of Wolf. In the name of Whale. In the name of Snake.

Forgive us. Have mercy. May they return. Not as a resurrection, but as living beings. Here. On this earth that is also theirs.

Oh Great Spirit. Please heal the animals. Please protect animals. Please restore the animals.

So our lives may also be healed. So our souls may also return. So our spirits may also be restored.

Oh spirit of Raven. Oh spirit of Wolf. Oh spirit of Whale. Oh spirit of Snake.

Teach us, again, how to live.

—*Deena Metzger*
THE SOUL OF NATURE

The Teaching Continues

By climbing up into his head and shutting out every voice but his own, "Civilized Man" has gone deaf. He can't hear the wolf calling him brother—not Master but brother. He can't hear the earth calling him child—not Father, but son. He hears only his own words making up the world. He can't hear the animals, they have nothing to say. Children babble and have to be taught how to climb up into their heads and shut the doors of perceptions. Only when the Man listens, and attends, O best Beloved, and hears, and understands, will the Cat return to the Cat's true silence.

—Ursula K. LeGuin
Buffalo Gals and Other Animal Presences

Authors tend to think of their books as children. We hold high hopes in our trembling hands for the future of these magical, literary offspring. I'll admit my hopes for the first edition of *Animals as Teachers & Healers* were implausibly grand, yet I have watched in utter amazement as this first child of mine rocketed itself into the world, leaving me behind, stunned, in its vapor trail.

If ever a book seemed to manifest a life and will of its own, surely this one has, finding homes for itself in niches I would never have imagined. Cancer patients tell me they use the book in their support groups. Nurses buy copies for their patients. One man said he read the book aloud for two full days to his beloved mare as she lay desperately sick with colic in a vet hospital. "She appreciated it, I could tell," he said. "And I know it helped us both." Parents tell me that they read stories from the book to their children at bedtime. A psychologist said she uses the book with some of her more withdrawn clients. She has discovered that stories of animals can draw out certain people who have mentally locked themselves away from healing.

Many people have told me how much the book assisted them in resolving painful issues surrounding their animal companions, especially those involving death and euthanasia. "Your book helped me to reconcile with the unexpected death of my little cat, Liesel, from cancer. Each story of a similar loss allowed me to cry and mourn for her. Thankfully, I don't feel as alone anymore with the pain, and that unbearable grief of holding her for the last time," wrote Kay Sassi, whose story about her dog, Sunshine, appears in the book. A wonderful man named Saul told me about the suffering he had endured for years regarding the death and burial of his beloved Saint Bernard. Buried in too shallow a grave, his dog was exhumed by predators, a horror Saul blamed on himself: "I have never been able to overcome the guilt that has so frequently brought me to tears of remorse and shame. As I laid your book down, a loud cry welled up and out of me. I had finally been able to let go."

Those who contributed to *Animals as Teachers & Healers* have become a large, extended family of sorts. Carol Maurillo, who is now working toward her degree in veterinary medicine, wrote, "I feel it is an honor and a privilege to be part of something so noble and full of truths. The people and the animals in the book are so real that they are now a part of my heart forever." Roger Fuchs, of "Fox Runs Away," echoed the joy that comes from seeing a moment of a lifetime preserved in the magic of the printed word: "Knowing that through my words part of the power of my experience lives even now in you, fifteen hundred miles from its setting and thirty years remote in time—I realize anew what power there is in words. The little red fox would be pleased." Jackie Geyer sends me regular updates on Chloé, the handstanding raccoon: "She showed up again this spring and there was this big brute of a fellow with her. I'm sure new babies are on the way."

The book has not only blazed a path of its own design—it has sent me out into the world, as well, to speak at workshops, readings, and conferences on the topic of animals as our mentors and healers. Always, these discussions focus on stories: those I tell, those I am told. I find that the simple telling of a story seems to cast a spell in a room, instantly creating a gentle air of intimacy and enchantment that warms even the most barren, cold meeting space. I believe it is vitally important that we share our personal stories with the world. In *Women Who Run With the Wolves*, Clarissa Pinkola Estés declares that "Stories are medicine. They do not require that we do, be, act anything—we need only listen. The remedies for repair or reclamation of any lost psychic drive are contained in stories." I have always held faith in the power of stories to heal and transform, and now, as I see *Animals as Teachers & Healers* work the magic of its stories within the hearts of its readers and contributors, my belief has become grounded in the rock-solid depth of experience. Now, more than ever, humankind needs to hear stories that are true and healing and vital. We need to become more steadfast believers in stories, too, and better listeners so that stories can find us, touch us, and mend us. We need to honor our own stories and truths about animals, and we need to listen to the stories animals have to tell us, as well. For within this sphere of heartfelt listening and sharing lies the soul of true communion with the animal nations—a deep and nurturing affection that can, I believe, restore our spirits and heal our earth.

Books

ANDREWS, TED. *Animalspeak.* A comprehensive guide to working with animal totems and spirits.

BOONE, JAY ALLEN. *Kinship With All Life.* A pioneer in the arena of interspecies communication, Boone was communing with his animal companions when Lassie had yet to be born. Boone's deep respect for all living beings shines.

BUFFALO HORN MAN, GARY. *Animal Energies.* This is a wonderful, pocket-size guide to the subtle energies inherent in specific animal species, based on the author's own experiences. Dancing Otter Publishing, P.O. Box 122, Sadieville, KY 40370.

FOX, MICHAEL W. *Eating with Conscience: The Bioethics of Food.* New Sage Press, 1997.

LEVINE, STEPHEN. *Healing Into Life and Death.* Addresses the theme of dying as a healing journey with great insight and compassion.

LOPEZ, BARRY. *Of Wolves and Men.* In my search for information about wolves, no book was more highly or frequently recommended to me. Thoroughly covers history, myth, politics, folklore, and biology.

MARTINO, TERESA TSIMMU. *The Wolf, the Woman, the Wilderness: A True Story of Returning Home* (Available Fall 1996, NewSage Press): A fascinating and adventurous story of returning a wolf to the wilderness, and in the process, the author's own journey in discovering her Native American roots.

Learning from Eagle, Living with Coyote. Wonderful poems with an enlightening cast of animal totems. Martino moves with grace and wisdom between the world of dream and spirit, and the world of daily convention.

METZGER, DEENA. *Looking for the Face of God.* Metzger is a poet, essayist, and novelist whose work is about creativity, transformation, and healing. Her poem, "Oh Great Spirit," has become a part of my nightly prayer ritual.

MURRAY, JOHN. *Out Among the Wolves, Contemporary Writings on the Wolf.* Some of the best contemporary writing about wolves and our evolving relationship with them.

PINKOLA ESTÉS, CLARISSA. *Women Who Run With the Wolves.* Story-laden celebration of the Wildwoman. An evocative, healing book with many animal images and myths.

SIEGEL, BERNIE. *Love, Medicine, & Miracles.* The first of several books about healing by Siegel, this remains my favorite anti-cancer textbook.

SMITH, KEITH. *Mourning Sickness.* A journey in words and paintings that follows the path of grief to healing, love, and personal growth. Rainbow Press, 30 Rainbow Trail, Sparta, NJ 07871

SMITH, PENELOPE. *Animals ... Our Return to Wholeness.* An acclaimed animal communication specialist, Smith writes convincingly about our ability to communicate with animals. Smith offers a wide variety of books, tapes, videos, seminars. Pegasus Publications, P.O. Box 1060, Point Reyes, CA 94956 or call (415) 663-1247.

TOBIAS, MICHAEL, AND COWAN, GEORGIANNE. *The Soul of Nature: Visions of a Living Earth.* This anthology discusses our responsibility to the natural world and all beings who share our planet.

Other Resources

Anaflora: Sharon Callahan is an animal communicator and healer who has developed a unique program of flower essence therapy for animals. Her work is gentle and intuitive, and highly effective. For more information write: P.O. Box 1056, Mt. Shasta, CA 96067, or call Sharon at (916) 926-6424.

Creation Spirituality Network: A magazine that explores pantheism: the belief that divinity permeates all living beings. Thoughtful articles by a wide range of writers. For information write: P.O. Box 20369, Oakland, CA 94620, (510) 654-2407.

Delphys: An organization that offers workshops, seminars, and writings to help people in their journey inward. Kim Rosen's work with dolphin and nature energy is inspiring. *Delphys* also has produced two musical recordings. For information write: P.O. Box 174, Bearsville, NY 12409

Delta Society: This nationwide organization is the best source for information about animal-assisted therapy and the use of service animals. Also, they publish a superb magazine dedicated to exploring human-animal interactions. For information, write: 289 Perimeter Road East, Renton, WA 98055, or call (425) 226-7357.

Dream Network: This journal contains a gold mine of information for those interested in working with dreams. For information write: Roberta Ossana, Editor, 1337 Powerhouse Lane, Moab, UT 84532.

Green Chimneys: The residential farm home combines at-risk and emotionally disturbed children with farm animals, birds of prey, and a vigorous riding program. The inspiring results have been documented in many national magazines and news shows. For more information write: Caller Box 719, Brewster, NY 10509, or call (914) 279-2995.

LaJoie Magazine: An uplifting, informal, bi-monthly collection of true stories that promote appreciation for animals of all kinds. For information write: Rita Reynolds, P.O. Box 145, Batesville, VA 22924

Medicine Cards: Available at many bookstores. Comes with a thorough guidebook by Jamie Sams and David Carson and a beautiful set of animal medicine cards. For more information write: Bear & Company, P.O. Drawer 2860, Sante Fe, NM 87504.

© Joey O'Brien

About the Author

A former technical writer and editor, SUSAN CHERNAK MCELROY has enjoyed a lifelong love affair with animals. Her enchantment with creatures great and small has been nurtured and strengthened through a lifetime of work with animals, first as a vet assistant, then zookeeper, humane educator, puppy trainer, kennel and stable hand, and wildlife rehabilitator. She currently lives with her husband and animal family on a small farm in Wyoming named Brightstar.

Susan McElroy lectures extensively and offers a series of audiotapes and workshops on animals as teachers and healers. If you would like information on these and other programs, or are interested in her newsletter, "Celebrating Animals as Teachers and Healers," please write Brightstar Farm, PO Box 13501, Jackson, Wyoming 83002. If you have a story to share, please include a stamped, self-addressed envelope.